How to Create a

BUTTERFLY
GARDEN

Also by Mathew Tekulsky

Americana: A Photographic Journey
Galapagos Birds: A Photographic Voyage
The Martin Luther King Mitzvah
The Art of Hummingbird Gardening
Backyard Bird Photography
Making Your Own Gourmet Coffee Drinks
Backyard Birdfeeding for Beginners

How to Create a
BUTTERFLY
GARDEN

Bringing the Beauty of Butterflies into Your World

WRITTEN AND PHOTOGRAPHED BY
MATHEW TEKULSKY

Skyhorse Publishing

Visit our website at www.skyhorsepublishing.com.

10 9 8 7 6 5 4 3 2 1

Library of Congress Cataloging-in-Publication Data is available on file.

Cover design by David Ter-Avanesyan
Cover photo credit: Mathew Tekulsky

Print ISBN: 978-1-5107-7140-6
Ebook ISBN: 978-1-5107-7154-3

Printed in China

To my mother, Patience Fish Tekulsky,
who accompanied me on many butterfly expeditions

Contents

Mathew Tekulsky photographing a Monarch butterfly
Author photograph by Patience Fish Tekulsky

Acknowledgments

At Skyhorse Publishing, I would like to thank my editor, Julie Ganz, and my publisher, Tony Lyons, for their continued encouragement and support.

Preface

This book was originally conceived in 1978, after I had discovered the pastime of attracting butterflies to one's garden. I had read about the subject in the magazine of a natural history museum, and I had also discovered that a gentleman named L. Hugh Newman had published a book called *Create a Butterfly Garden* back in 1967. He had supplied Sir Winston Churchill's garden and butterfly house at Churchill's Chartwell estate with thousands of butterflies over the years, and he had decided to write a book about how you could enjoy the beauty of butterflies in your own backyard, as he did in his own butterfly garden in Kent, England. Well, I'm glad that Mr. Newman wrote that book because it inspired me to be the first author in North America to write a book about butterfly gardening.

But it would not be easy. In the first place, most of the publishers that my literary agent Jane Jordan Browne approached with my idea considered the subject unworthy of book form, relegating it to magazine article status. I, of course disagreed, and one day shortly after I put together my proposal and outline, I was ushered into the offices of an editor at the Harper & Row publishing house in New York City. The editor heard me out on the subject, but would not make me a publishing offer unless I wrote the first two chapters of the book for him as a sample. There was only one problem. I knew virtually nothing about butterfly gardening!

I told Jane that I could not research the subject without spending at least three months doing bookwork and fieldwork, and I declined the offer from Harper & Row, as I was just barely making ends meet as a newspaper and magazine writer at the time and I could not afford to take unpaid time off on speculation for an editor who made no guarantees and on a subject that I knew practically nothing about.

So I put the idea away and basically forgot about it. Then, one day in 1984, I was sitting in my furnished studio apartment in West Los Angeles when the phone rang.

"Hello, Mathew?" a woman's voice on the other end of the line said.

"Yes," I answered.

"It's Jane Browne," the voice said.

I was irritated and I thought, well, what does she want? Probably another rejection of that butterfly gardening proposal. Instead, it was quite the opposite.

"I have an offer for the butterfly gardening book from the Harvard Common Press," she said.

As any good author would reply, I said the first thing that came into my mind.

"How much?" I said, referring to the advance against royalties.

"Two thousand. Five hundred on signing, five hundred on delivery of the outline and one chapter, and the rest on delivery and acceptance of the manuscript."

I did a bit of quick math in my head and I realized that I would be spending the next year of my life doing this book for $2,000, minus the agent's commission of ten percent (they now get fifteen), and minus taxes, if there were any, not to mention any and all expenses that I would incur if I agreed to undertake the project.

"Well," I said, "I guess I have to do it."

Jane agreed, and I was off to the races. Since I was living in a one-room apartment with no garden of my own, I had to figure out how to write the book without being surrounded by butterflies all day long.

The first thing I did was rush to a used bookstore and gather up all of the books about butterflies that I could find. The first and most important of these books was *The Butterflies of North America*, edited and illustrated by William H. Howe. This book included an introduction that explained the biology and life cycle of butterflies, and it also had species accounts and illustrations of 2,093 butterflies. The species accounts included descriptions of each butterfly from egg to caterpillar to chrysalis to adult; information about their habits; their range of distribution; and when during the year they were on the wing. I was in butterfly heaven, and I devoured the descriptions in the text as well as the illustrations as I tried to imbue myself with as much information about butterflies as I could from that book.

Over the next few months, I spent countless hours looking up articles about butterflies in the biological journals that were housed at the UCLA Biomedical Library in Westwood. I photocopied hundreds and hundreds of pages, and hurried home to my apartment to scour them for information about my favorite topic. Some of these articles, such as Henry George Heal's piece about the Drum Manor Butterfly Garden in Northern Ireland, transported me to exotic locations, and I could imagine being there and having all of these wonderful butterflies fluttering about my head. I felt calm and contented just to be researching this marvelous material, and I couldn't wait to write it up for my future readers. Plus, I needed that advance money.

As I continued my research for the book, I took many local field trips to places where I knew butterflies would be, such as botanical gardens and a few private residences. I also did a lot of fieldwork around West Los Angeles and Santa Monica, where I saw the Cabbage White, Anise Swallowtail, and Gulf Fritillary, as well as Monarchs flying among the flowers on tree-lined streets. I also learned to identify the caterpillars of the Anise Swallowtail, which first appear as tiny black specks on the fennel that often grows on the side of the road; and the eggs of the Cabbage White, which I discovered on the undersides of nasturtium leaves. I found Monarch caterpillars on milkweed plants and Gulf Fritillary caterpillars on the leaves of their only foodplant, passion flower, which grows along fences throughout Los Angeles.

After a few months of research, I started writing the book, describing the life cycle of the butterfly, where and when they were on the wing, how to set up your butterfly garden, the nectar sources and larval foodplants that butterflies use, and a number of butterfly gardening activities you can do. When I reached the chapter on how to rear butterflies, I realized that I would have to conduct this eccentric activity in my apartment!

I gathered some cardboard boxes and placed the foodplants of the Anise Swallowtail, Gulf Fritillary, Cabbage White, and Monarch in each of them, respectively. Then I placed a stick in each box and covered the stick and the box with fine-mesh netting. I put some caterpillars of each species into each of the boxes and watched the caterpillars grow into late-stage larvae that would eventually pupate and hang from the sticks that I had provided in each box. When the butterflies emerged, I took them outside and released them on the street outside of my apartment building.

The interesting thing about this process, which took a couple of months, was that I lived on the second (and top) floor of an apartment building that surrounded a patio that had a pool and some lounge chairs, one of which was used every day by the apartment manager, an elderly woman who sunbathed in a bikini until her skin was dark. She greeted me every day as I came in and out of my apartment with the words, "Have a good one," and I never told her that I was raising a virtual zoo of flying insects in the apartment above that patio! I also had to keep my windows shut so that the noise of my typewriter wouldn't bother my neighbors. But I endured it all because I loved my subject, and I wanted to get my first book published. And in 1985, that is exactly what happened.

The book sold well for many years, but eventually, it fell out of print. Then, in 2014, Skyhorse Publishing offered to reprint *The Butterfly Garden* as long as I provided them with photographs of butterflies to supplement the text. (The original book had black-and-white illustrations.) So I took out my macro lenses, put them on my Canon 7D camera bodies, and rushed out to find as many butterflies as I could to photograph for the new edition.

As it happened, my first publisher had altered my original text just before publication, as there was concern that the book was too erudite to be serialized in magazines such as *Better Homes & Gardens*. In fact, the text had been rewritten in order to, in their opinion, make it easier to read for a wider audience. Fortunately, I had saved the original galleys, which contained the typeset text that I had handed in and which had been accepted before it was changed at the last minute. For the Skyhorse edition, I polished and edited my original text from these galleys until the book became what it is today. I am extremely pleased that I was able to rescue my original version of this book.

The Art of Butterfly Gardening was published in 2015, and I am very happy with it. But now, since it is the thirty-eighth anniversary of the original publication of *The Butterfly Garden*, Skyhorse Publishing and I have decided to give my beloved butterfly gardening book a relaunch. As a tribute to L. Hugh Newman's book, my initial inspiration for this journey, we are calling this special edition *How to Create a Butterfly Garden*, and I hope that it inspires more and more people to not only observe these wonderful creatures of the air but to plant gardens that will attract them and contribute to their preservation.

Sadly, in the years since *The Butterfly Garden* was published, the populations and habitat of butterfly species throughout North America have dwindled precipitously, especially for the magnificent Monarch Butterfly. This is primarily due to loss of habitat, the use of herbicides and pesticides, and climate change, including drought. In addition, for an already dwindling population of migratory butterflies, the effect of unpredictable and severe weather events such as heavy rains and wildfires can be devastating.

To counteract this alarming trend, numerous conservation groups have banded together to save populations of migratory Monarchs by protecting their overwintering and breeding sites by planting thousands of milkweed plants along the Monarch's traveling route, so that the Monarch caterpillars will have something to eat, and by planting nectar sources for the adult Monarchs and other species of butterflies.

Butterfly gardeners can contribute to this effort by planting flowers that do not require much water and have not been treated with pesticides. Furthermore, if you have a variety of blossoms in your garden from early spring through late summer, migrating Monarchs will be able to nectar on your flowers if the butterflies arrive early in the spring on their northward journey, as well as when they embark southward on their fall migration.

Butterfly gardeners may also want to help protect known Monarch habitat in their own neighborhoods, such as patches of milkweed and groves of trees where the Monarchs can overwinter; and they can also participate in activities that involve observing and documenting milk-weed plants and Monarchs throughout North America and reporting these observations to organizations that maintain databases that can be used to convince policymakers to protect the Monarchs as well as the plants that these marvelous insects need in order to survive.

In addition to butterfly gardens at people's homes, butterfly gardens can be created at schools, libraries, parks, nature centers, zoos, botanical gardens, natural history museums, and even at businesses that have land available for this purpose.

When *The Butterfly Garden* was first published back in 1985, there were few if any butterfly houses or gardens in North America that were open to the public. Today, there are butterfly gardens, houses, exhibits, and displays all over North America, and I would like to think that my little book played a not insignificant role in increasing the popularity of butterflies that continues to this day and will hopefully grow well into the future.

There is something about butterflies that makes me calm and medi-tative when I am around these silent, airborne creatures. They drift through the sky and flutter around me, and all I can do is look out at them in wonder . . . wonder at how they came into this world in the first place, wonder at how they have managed to survive for so long in a perilous environment, and wonder at how we can manage to save them from falling by the wayside of evolution.

—Mathew Tekulsky, Los Angeles, 2023

Zebra Heliconian

CHAPTER 1

What Is Butterfly Gardening?

It is a calm, sunny afternoon, with a hint of a breeze. You are standing in a meadow, rich with flowers of red, orange, purple, and yellow. Suddenly, over a row of daisies, a Monarch butterfly appears. The orange and black Monarch flaps its wings, changes direction, and settles onto the ball-shaped flower head of a buttonbush. Immediately it unrolls its proboscis and starts to feed from the scores of tiny white flowers. A few minutes later, it flies away, disappearing over a bed of lavender.

Monarch

Butterflies, such as the Monarch, epitomize all that is ethereal, peaceful, and free. Wild creatures, they inhabit a domain that existed for millions of years without man. But, like some birds, certain butterflies have adapted to human changes and are able to flourish in rural areas, towns, and cities. Thus, you don't have to visit the far reaches of the countryside to enjoy the combined beauty of butterflies and flowers. You can create scenes like the one described above right in your own garden. Whether you live on a farm or in the city, all you have to do to attract butterflies is to cultivate plants they like.

Wherever you live, you have a chance to see butterflies: on mountains, by the seashore, across prairies, in swamps and forests, even in deserts. And wherever butterflies occur, butterfly gardening may be practiced. By knowing their needs and accommodating them, you can plan and predict which butterflies will appear. If you have a suburban yard, butterfly gardening is an ideal way to add some color to the neighborhood. If your neighbors join in, the whole block can be changed for the better and brighter. The limits lie in your imagination and the preferences of the butterflies themselves.

People have been enjoying butterfly gardening for as long as butterflies, plants, and humans have coexisted. One of the earliest butterfly gardeners was Aristotle, who described the life history of the Cabbage White. In 1912, Charles McGlashan and his daughter Ximena started a "butterfly farm" in Truckee, California, as a way for Ximena to make money by collecting and rearing butterflies for sale. The business blossomed, and Ximena became the toast of the press, which dubbed her "The Butterfly Queen." A year later, the McGlashans started a publication called *The Butterfly Farmer: A Monthly Magazine for Amateur Entomologists.* The magazine contained information on how to raise butterflies, as well as directions for pinning, mounting and preserving specimens. Ximena used the money toward a degree in botany and entomology from Stanford University in 1915. She soon married, and butterfly farming took a back seat to raising her family.

In the early 1930s, Albert Carter and his wife Amy raised as many as 16,000 butterflies at one time in a 100-square-foot, screened-in hillside area which they called Butterfly Park. Located in Sunland, California, the park was open to visitors, for free, and included labeled plants, waterfalls, picnic tables, and peacocks. For a number of years, the Carters published a magazine called *Butterfly Park Nature Club News,* which, like the McGlashans's journal, provided information on how to raise butterflies for fun and profit. In addition to specimens, the Carters sold trays, jewelry, and other items that they decorated with butterflies. The park was closed in 1935.

Perhaps the modern world's most famous butterfly gardener was Sir Winston Churchill. In the spring of 1939, Churchill decided to start a butterfly garden at his Chartwell estate and enlisted the help of L. Hugh Newman and Newman's father, who had founded a butterfly farm nearby to provide butterflies to the public. However, World War II broke out a few months later, and it wasn't until 1946 that Churchill was able to make his butterfly garden a reality. Newman supplied the garden with more than eleven species, including the Red Admiral and Painted Lady (which also occur in North America), as well as British species such as the Peacock, Brimstone, and Small Tortoiseshell. For several years, he provided 1,000 to 1,500 butterflies per year. In 1947, Newman released about 200 Small Tortoiseshells and Peacocks on the grounds so that people attending a political garden party the next day could enjoy the butterflies fluttering around the valerians and other flowers. Churchill even had a summerhouse converted into a butterfly house and spent many hours inside it, watching different types of butterflies emerge from their chrysalises.

Newman notes that Churchill "carefully avoided killing a single insect. It was live butterflies he wanted to see flying in his garden and in the park." He goes on to say that Churchill wanted to increase the number of butterflies in his immediate neighborhood as well. "I am certain," he concludes, "that during the years when I was regularly turning out specially bred or surplus stock for Chartwell there was a great resurgence of the butterfly population in that part of Kent—thanks to Mr. Churchill."

In order to have your own butterfly garden, you don't have to go to Churchill's extremes. In fact, you can begin with very little effort and expense. All you need are plants for the adult butterflies (nectar sources) and plants for the caterpillars (larval foodplants).

Butterflies sip the nectar of many flowers throughout the day, by sucking through a tube called a proboscis, which they uncoil from under their heads. Just as we relish the taste of honeysuckle nectar, so do butterflies. Many nectar sources have flat heads consisting of numerous tiny florets (such as daisies); others have a cluster of small flowers in a dome, or along a spike.

Some butterflies are attracted to a wide range of nectar sources. Others, because of the size, shape, or color of the flower, express definite preferences. For instance, the Eastern Tailed–Blue, a small butterfly

Giant Swallowtail

with a short proboscis, prefers short-tubed or open flowers such as clover, cinquefoil, and fleabane. However, the Spicebush Swallowtail, a large butterfly with a long proboscis, likes long-tubed flowers such as Japanese honeysuckle and jewelweed. And although butterflies are drawn to flowers of all colors, the Pearl Crescent is fond of white and yellow flowers, while the Silver-spotted Skipper is especially attracted to purple ones.

Butterflies are much more selective toward their larval foodplants. Because of certain chemical constituents in the leaves of plants, caterpillars of particular species of butterflies will feed only on plants containing those chemicals. If for some reason the caterpillar wanders away from its foodplant, it will starve to death rather than eat the wrong host.

Why does this happen? Paul Ehrlich and Peter Raven suggest that it is due to the "coevolution" of plants and the animals that feed on them. Ehrlich and Raven contend that as a defense mechanism, plants have developed certain chemicals that are repellant to most insects. However, some insects (including caterpillars) have become so adapted to cope with these substances that they actually come to require them. Through this interaction, diverse species of plants and insects have evolved. By specializing in this way, insects reduce their competition and carve out a special niche.

For instance, caterpillars of a group of butterflies called whites are drawn to mustard oils contained in plants of the mustard and caper families. These chemicals repel most other herbivorous insects. Similarly, three essential oils present in plants of the citrus and parsley families serve to attract a number of swallowtail caterpillars. Ehrlich and Raven point out that these two plant families have not been considered related, but that this chemical evidence suggests that they are. Thus, butterflies may be better botanists than humans.

Indeed, Samuel Hubbard Scudder, in his classic work *Frail Children of the Air,* titles one of his chapters "Butterflies as Botanists." In it he states, "In many, perhaps the majority of instances the plants upon which allied species or genera of caterpillars feed, themselves belong to allied families of the botanical systems." Scudder then cites German botanist Fritz Muller, who "brings forward some curious instances in which a knowledge of the habits of butterflies would have led, had they been followed, to an earlier recognition of the affinities of certain plants."

In one of his examples, Muller explains that two genera of butterflies, *Ageronia* (now *Hamadryas*) and *Didonis* (now *Biblis*), were once considered to be widely separated, even distinct families, "but now they are to be found beside one another among the subfamily Nymphalinae, and the structure of their caterpillars leaves no doubt about their close affinity." Muller points out that *Ageronia* caterpillars feed on *Dalechampia,* and *Didonis* larvae feed on *Tragia*. Then he notes that these two plant genera, once widely separated, have recently been placed close together in Bentham and Hooker's *Genera Plantamm*. "Thus their close affinity which had been duly appreciated by butterflies has finally been recognized by botanists also."

Caterpillars, therefore, can be very picky eaters. Some, such as the Painted Lady and Gray Hairstreak, accept a wider range of plants than others, but most stick to a few related plants or a single species. This is a boon to gardeners, who may worry that their favorite flowers will be damaged. Furthermore, most caterpillars do not attack garden plants to any significant degree. Farmers, of course, are familiar with the Cabbage White and Orange Sulphur, and you may have to plant some extra cabbage, nasturtium, or alfalfa to make sure there's enough for the butterflies and yourself. This is a small price to pay for the pleasure they provide.

One butterfly gardener in Massachusetts shares her parsley with larvae of the Black Swallowtail. "It makes a lovely border," she states, "and there is always enough for both butterflies and people." She adds that other wild and cultivated members of the carrot family can be used with butterflies in the Black Swallowtail group. Meanwhile, in Pasadena, California, a butterfly gardener has provided a number of large fennel plants for the Anise Swallowtail and he still has more than enough of this tasty herb to spice up his salads. He also grows extra radishes and broccoli for the Cabbage White.

Sometimes, caterpillar infestations occur. The Mourning Cloak, for instance, lays its eggs in clusters, and its caterpillars can decimate the branches of an elm or willow tree. One butterfly gardener recalled having so many Gulf Fritillary caterpillars on her passion flower that they were falling on her head. Situations like this, however, are rare. If you have too many caterpillars, the best thing is to transfer them to a plant some distance from your yard. In a natural garden, predators and parasitoids such as spiders, wasps, ants, flies, and beetles will keep caterpillars under control. What they don't get, birds, small mammals, and inclement weather will. Natural gardens are infinitely more interesting than their sterile counterparts. Ironically, by excluding predators, sprayed gardens actually encourage pests.

In some cases, butterflies are effective aids in weed control. During mass migrations, Monarchs devour millions of milkweeds. Painted Ladies cut back wide areas of thistles when they colonize North America each spring. The Red Admiral, Eastern Comma, Satyr Comma, and Milbert's Tortoiseshell consume countless patches of stinging nettles. The Fiery Skipper will even trim your Bermuda grass for you.

If the caterpillars in your yard become too numerous, the adults of that species may notice and lay their eggs elsewhere. V. G. Dethier and Robert MacArthur studied a field's capacity to support a population of Harris' Checkerspots. They added 19,800 caterpillars in the autumn of one year (25 times the number already there), and the following autumn, the number had fallen to 400, "which is about what it would have been had there been no new larvae introduced." Dethier and MacArthur observed that the butterflies laid far fewer eggs in the field that second year, choosing asters along a nearby road instead. They concluded that the controlling factor on the caterpillar population was the movement of adults into and out of the field.

When a caterpillar becomes full-grown, it turns into a chrysalis, and a number of days or even months later, a butterfly emerges. If you have plenty of nectar sources on hand, it may enjoy its first meal in your garden and will perhaps remain in your yard. That completes the cycle of butterfly gardening—butterflies arrive, feed, reproduce, and remain. The most successful butterfly gardens contain a good variety of foodplants and nectar sources. You can attract butterflies with some of their favorite nectar flowers, and then have the foodplants on hand so the females can lay their eggs. Or the reverse can occur. The presence of nectar flowers and larval foodplants will attract females, which may in turn attract males. With proper resources available, visiting butterflies may establish a colony in your backyard.

Perhaps the best and easiest way to get started as a butterfly gardener is to observe what's going on in your neighborhood. Keep your eyes open for which butterflies are on the wing. Conduct a local survey to determine which flowers they choose for nectar and which larval foodplants they prefer. Be sure to visit local fields and forests, as well as nearby gardens and parks. Certain butterflies and flowers are more plentiful during some months than others, so make your observations at different times of the year. With this information, you can determine which butterflies use which plants in each season.

By consulting a national or regional butterfly field guide, you'll learn to identify many butterflies. Before long, you'll recognize them without referring to the book. If they're around, that means their foodplant probably occurs nearby. In Southern California, fennel (or anise) grows as a common roadside and canyon plant. This licorice-tasting herb can be found in the supermarket and serves as a foodplant for the Anise Swallowtail. Fennel can just as easily be grown in your garden as by the side of the road. All you have to do is obtain seeds from a nursery or a wild plant, and cultivate them. Once you have the fennel in your yard, chances are you'll be able to watch from close up as an Anise Swallowtail lays her eggs. Or if you live in the eastern half of the country, just substitute Black Swallowtails and dill and have the same experience.

Butterfly gardens come in all shapes and sizes. They are as diverse as the people who create them. Your own butterfly garden can be as simple or as challenging as you want. For example, in addition to attracting lots of different butterflies to your daisies, you may wish to bring in a great many of just one or two species—perhaps because you like the way they look, or you'd like to learn more about them, or they're the most common so they'll be the easiest to attract. Whatever the reason, plant the foodplant for that butterfly and you may well get what you want. If you wish to harbor a rarer species, you can plant its foodplant and see if it will come. That's part of the challenge.

Butterflies, however, can be unpredictable. Clouded Sulphurs may fill up your garden one year and be not so common the next. You may not have White Admirals for a year or two, and suddenly your yard will be brimming with them. Where, when, and how many butterflies turn up at a given place depends on where the females lay their eggs (some can lay hundreds in one spot); how the weather affects butterflies' survival rates and emergence times; and a host of other factors, not to mention pure chance. Indeed, you may think the world has run out of Silvery Blues, only to discover that the fellow down the street has a colony in his garden.

One of the deepest rewards of gardening with butterflies is that it gives you an opportunity to experience firsthand the wonder and magic of nature. In addition to watching the butterflies in your garden, you'll be exposed to a whole world of marvelous creatures and arresting activities. You'll no doubt see bees collecting nectar from flowers; spiders setting their traps and waiting for prey; colorful insects of many forms on flower heads and other parts of plants; dragonflies hawking around—a whole range of activity, all interconnected. Birds fly overhead, in search of food (which includes caterpillars and butterflies), and many a butterfly gardener has seen his cat jump three feet into the air to try and catch a butterfly. One butterfly gardener reported that her cat never killed the butterfly, but pinned its wings to the ground with its paws. Upon being released, the butterfly soared into the air, unharmed. She added that butterflies often swoop down close to her cat, as if playing a game of "catch me if you can."

Butterfly gardening brings other rewards. In this age of increased urbanization and destruction of our open areas, butterfly gardeners can help populations of butterflies to remain stable and even increase in areas where they have been adversely affected. Occasionally, this might include helping to save a rare and endangered species. But even some common butterflies have become rarer in the cities than they once were. Butterfly gardeners can help bring them back to their former numbers. Although nature reserves are generally thought of as the vehicles for this type of conservation, it is possible that one of the largest and most effective "reserves" in the country is the total area of all the gardens at people's homes.

Denis Owen, a British biologist, recorded almost a quarter of all British butterfly species in his Leicester garden. He notes that in 1972, nature reserves in England and Wales comprised 85,000 acres, while suburban gardens accounted for about a million acres, or about 1/37 of the total land area. Owen adds that suburbia, with its rich diversity of native and exotic plants supporting "an almost incredible variety" of insect species, is expanding.

Since most rare butterfly species do not occur in gardens, it may be an exaggeration to suggest that gardens can play a primary role in conserving the diversity of species found in the wild. However, gardens do support many butterfly species that are affected by the destruction of natural habitats. If we use gardens to help wildlife, we can not only enjoy the fulfillment of having contributed something to our environment; we can enjoy the evidence of it every day.

At one time, I was an apartment dweller, and I did not have a butterfly garden of my own. No one at my apartment building made a conscious attempt to attract butterflies. And yet, the hibiscus out front supported a small colony of Gray Hairstreaks, and the lawn was inhabited by Fiery Skippers. Two houses away, female Cabbage Whites constantly laid their eggs on the nasturtiums by the sidewalk. I brought some of these leaves in, reared the caterpillars until they pupated, and then released the newly hatched butterflies into the area around the nasturtiums. There was a passion flower nearby, and I almost became addicted to rearing Gulf Fritillaries, releasing them five at a time on occasion. I reared a number of Monarchs and Anise Swallowtails in that apartment as well. So even though I didn't have a butterfly garden, I had plenty of butterfly activity. In addition, the elms down the street supported a number of Mourning Cloaks, and I occasionally saw a Checkered White, Sleepy Orange, or Western Tiger Swallowtail drinking nectar at the coreopsis, sweet alyssum, and geraniums in the neighborhood.

I have visited many butterfly gardens. When I stand in one, it is not hard to convince myself that butterflies lead a charmed existence. It's like being out in a mountain meadow, with all this peace and beauty around

Gulf Fritillary

Anise Swallowtail

Checkered White

me. Historically, I know I am not alone. In his autobiography, *Speak, Memory,* novelist Vladimir Nabokov recalls the wonderful times he had with butterflies in the garden and surrounding countryside at his family's summer home near St. Petersburg. "From the age of seven, everything I felt in connection with a rectangle of framed sunlight was dominated by a single passion. If my first glance of the morning was for the sun, my first thought was for the butterflies it would engender. . . . On the honeysuckle, overhanging the carved back of a bench just opposite the main entrance, my guiding angel . . . pointed out to me a rare visitor, a splendid, pale-yellow creature with black blotches, blue crenels, and a cinnabar eyespot above each chrome-rimmed black tail. As it probed the inclined flower from which it hung, its powdery body slightly bent, it kept restlessly jerking its great wings, and my desire for it was one of the most intense I have ever experienced." Nabokov later became a renowned lepidopterist and he named, among other butterflies, the Karner Blue (a subspecies of the Melissa Blue), which exists in various parts of the northern Midwest and Northeast and is on the endangered species list.

It is not surprising that writers and artists find inspiration in the combination of butterflies and flowers. Both seem to appear from out of nowhere. Then there's the excitement of seeing the beauty of a butterfly suddenly combined with that of a flower. It is a vision that can be enjoyed for that moment and remembered for years. In a way, if you have a butterfly garden, you can live as charmed an existence as the butterflies do: at least for the time you share with them. And that, really, is what butterfly gardening is all about.

Nabokov explains this feeling perhaps as eloquently as one can: "I confess I do not believe in time. . . . And the highest enjoyment of timelessness . . . is when I stand among rare butterflies and their food plants. This is ecstasy, and behind the ecstasy is something else, which is hard to explain. It is like a momentary vacuum into which rushes all that I love. A sense of oneness with sun and stone. A thrill of gratitude to whom it may concern—to the contrapuntal genius of human fate or to tender ghosts humoring a lucky mortal."

Giant Swallowtails

CHAPTER 2

Butterfly Lives

In 1955, William H. Howe, author of *The Butterflies of North America,* collected 64 butterfly species on his nine-acre farm in Ottawa, Kansas. Howe's list, reported in *The Lepidopterists' News,* contains 31 of the butterflies in our "Fifty North American Garden Butterflies" section— including the Monarch, Mourning Cloak, Painted Lady, Buckeye, Red-spotted Purple, and Eastern Tiger Swallowtail. It also features a number of other common species, such as the Variegated Fritillary, Gray Comma, Goatweed Leafwing, Little Yellow, and Eastern Tailed-Blue. Howe notes that he collected an additional 18 species within a mile of his farm. "And this does not include some skippers I cannot positively identify!"

There are indeed a great number of butterfly species—approximately 20,000 species worldwide, and about 725 species in North America north of Mexico. Butterflies are often distinguished by their wing colors. Major groups include the whites and sulphurs, blues and coppers, browns (or satyrs), yellow-and-black swallowtails, and orange butterflies, such as the fritillaries. Beyond primary coloration is the pattern of colors on the wings, and the shape of the wings themselves. Hairstreaks have streaky lines on their underwings, and usually have one or two thin tails extending from each hindwing. Checkerspots have varying, checkered patterns of black, brown, orange, yellow, and white. Crescents have oval, pearly or silvery spots on their underwings, as do many fritillaries and checkerspots. Metalmarks are characterized by thin, metallic borders on their wings. Longwings, such as the Julia Heliconian, have a wide wingspan and narrow, curved wings. Many skippers look like fighter planes and dart or skip around close to the ground. Swallowtails have a tail on

Orange-barred Sulphur

Julia Heliconian

the end of each wing, and the Two-tailed Swallowtail has two of them. There's even a Three-tailed Swallowtail, which occasionally visits Texas and Arizona from Mexico.

Within each group or family of butterflies, each species has its own characteristics. Anglewings, such as the Eastern Comma and Question Mark, are named for their jagged, angular wings. However, the Eastern Comma has a silver comma mark on the underside of each hindwing, and the Question Mark has a dot below the comma, thus forming a question mark. Because of their unique coloration, some butterflies almost defy being categorized. These include the Common Buckeye, with its shiny, bluish-purple eyespots set against a tawny-brown background; the Red Admiral, with orange-red bars on a black backdrop; the Mourning Cloak, with a creamy-yellow border, bluish-violet spots, and a dark mahogany background; and the Monarch, with its distinctive orange and black pattern.

Butterflies vary greatly in many other aspects besides their wings. While the Gulf Fritillary's proboscis is a light-brown color, that of the Anise Swallowtail is shiny and black. Furthermore, it has shiny black eyes compared with the orange eyes of the Gulf Fritillary or the light-green ones of the Cabbage White. In many butterflies, such as the whites, sulphurs, and swallowtails, all six legs are fully developed. But the nymphalids, which comprise almost a third of all North American species (including many of the more common and conspicuous butterflies), have stunted front legs that barely reach the end of their "chest." Hence, they are called "brush-footed butterflies."

In many butterfly species, the male and female look different. The males of most blues have bright-blue wings, whereas the females are often brown or gray. The male Black Swallowtail is yellow and black, but the female is mostly black and blue and mimics the Pipevine Swallowtail. Female Eastern Tiger Swallowtails have two forms: the yellow-and-black form, which resembles the male, and a black variety, common in the South, that also mimics the Pipevine Swallowtail.

Other butterflies vary from season to season. The Eastern Comma and Question Mark have a summer form with dark hindwings, and a fall form with orange hindwings. The spring form of the Zebra Swallowtail is smaller, paler, and has tails half the length of the summer individuals. Some members of the same species exhibit regional differences. For instance, the Viceroy, which mimics the Monarch in most of its range, has a darker, mahogany-brown form in the Deep South, where it mimics the Queen.

Butterflies go through four distinct stages in their life cycle—egg, or ovum (plural, ova); caterpillar, or larva (plural, larvae); chrysalis, or pupa (plural, pupae); and adult, or imago (plural, imagoes). In each of these stages, each butterfly species has its own distinctive appearance. In fact, it is often possible to identify a species by observing its early forms. Some field guides have illustrations of caterpillars, chrysalises, and even eggs, but you can also learn to identify these early stages through personal observation and rearing. Although many caterpillars look similar, especially within the same group or family, larvae as a whole exhibit a great variety of shapes, colors, and sizes. For example, the Boisduval's Blue caterpillar, 3/8″ long, is green, sluglike, and covered with short white hairs. The black and orange Baltimore Checkerspot, 1″ in length, is covered with black spines. The Black Swallowtail larva is 2″ long, and each segment of its green body has a black band with yellow or orange spots.

The shape and coloring of chrysalises also varies from species to species. You can learn to recognize chrysalises as well as adults, just as you tell a plant by its leaf or flower. For instance, the chrysalis of the Mourning Cloak hangs upside down and has a number of thorny spines along its light-brown body. The Variegated Fritillary also hangs upside down, but this pupa is a pearly blue-green with black, orange, yellow, and gold spots. The Falcate Orangetip looks like a long, green bud and hangs rightside up, supported by a silken girdle. Even the texture of pupal cases is distinctive. The Monarch's case is of a clear, smooth, waferlike material that crackles like thin plastic when the butterfly emerges. The Gulf Fritillary's case is more like thin bark or a leaf and is virtually silent during eclosure.

It is clear, then, that butterflies exhibit wide differences in appearance from one species to the next. But they are still all butterflies, as distinguished from their co-members of the order Lepidoptera—moths.

The name Lepidoptera is derived from the Greek words *lepis* (scale) and *ptera* (wing). Both butterflies and moths have scaly wings. But while butterflies have clubbed antennae (with a swelling at the tip), moth antennae, whether slim or feathery, taper to a fine point. Most butterfly bodies are slender and bare; most moths have thick, hairy bodies. When at rest, butterflies generally hold their wings upright over their backs; moths tend to hold them out flat. Butterflies fly during the day; most moths fly at night. Most butterflies (except for the skippers) have a naked chrysalis; most moths spin a cocoon in which the pupa rests until emergence. Moth larvae are similar to butterfly larvae, however, in that they too are wormlike and feed on the leaves of various trees, shrubs, and herbs. Indeed, you may wish to garden for moths as well as for butterflies. If so, you have plenty from which to choose. There are at least ten times as many moth species as butterflies.

All butterflies begin life as an egg, which is laid by the female on a leaf or flower head of a plant. Females begin laying eggs within hours of mating, and may continue over a number of days or weeks. The female senses the right plant before she even lays the egg. Sight and pattern recognition certainly play a role in identifying the proper host. However, Scudder raises an interesting question: "Pray how does the green of one plant differ from that of all others?" Scudder states that smell is the primary sense used to detect the right host. Scent, of course, is an important ingredient in mate attraction, as both male and female butterflies produce such odors. Since plants also produce odors, it is only logical to conclude that when the female engages in her characteristic egg-laying flight—fluttering from one plant to the next, and finally landing on the correct host—her actions are based on the sense of smell.

However, taste also plays an important role in this process. Butterflies smell with their antennae and palpi (furry appendages on either side of the proboscis), but they taste with the tarsi of their hind legs. By scratching the leaves of plants with their tarsi, females can sense the chemicals in those plants to determine whether they have found the appropriate host. This is similar to the process by which butterflies recognize the presence of sugar in water. Biologist E. B. Ford reports that a butterfly almost always unrolls its proboscis when one of its hind legs is immersed in water to which apple juice has been added. However, it only unrolls its proboscis about once in three times when the tarsus is not immersed in the liquid. Ford concludes that "while the butterfly is capable of perceiving the scent of the juice, it is much more stimulated if it can touch it." But mere touch is not enough to elicit the proper response, he states, "since the immersion of the susceptible tarsus in plain water has no effect, even when the insect is allowed to smell the apple juice as before." How sensitive is a butterfly's sense of taste? The Monarch responds to sugar solutions of .0003 percent, which corresponds to a taste sensitivity 2,408 times greater than that of humans.

When the female finds the proper foodplant, she flutters above it, gently drops down and, while resting briefly on a leaf, stem, or flower head, swings her abdomen up and deposits a moist, glistening, circular or oblong egg. Some butterflies, such as the Pearl Crescent, Baltimore Checkerspot, Mourning Cloak, and Pipevine Swallowtail lay their eggs in small groups or in clusters of hundreds. Others, such as the Eastern Comma and Question Mark, lay their eggs in vertical columns of three to ten eggs. Some, such as the Great Spangled Fritillary, lay their eggs

Monarch laying an egg

Monarch egg

Pipevine Swallowtail eggs

near, as well as on the foodplant, while some of the browns simply drop their eggs haphazardly in the vicinity of the foodplant. Most butterflies, however, lay their eggs singly, and they usually place the egg on the underside of the leaf, so as to afford it protection.

Butterfly eggs vary in appearance from species to species, and even change color over time. When just laid, a Gulf Fritillary egg is light-yellow, oblong, and has longitudinal striations. The next day, it turns amber and remains darkened until it hatches. The egg of a Cabbage White is similar in shape, but smaller and whiter and it remains white until hatching. An Eastern Tiger Swallowtail's eggs are yellow-green and spherical, while a Mourning Cloak's are keg-shaped, pale, and turn black before hatching. Most eggs are less than a millimeter in diameter and hatch within a few days or a week, releasing a minute caterpillar. But the eggs of some species overwinter, and in some cases, as with certain swallowtails and blues, the eggs can wait two or more years before hatching.

The first thing most caterpillars do is eat their eggshell, thus making efficient use of available resources. Then they start wandering around the leaf, nibbling the tender areas until their mouthparts have hardened. Often they gravitate to the edge of the leaf, where they can get a good start. Soon they attack the full leaf, feeding in distinctive patterns according to their kind.

A caterpillar *is* a butterfly in another stage. It has a large head with a hard shell or capsule around it. Each side of the head contains a group of simple eyes, or ocelli. The head also has a pair of antennae, a silk spinneret on the lower "lip," and a pair of mandibles which it uses for chewing its food. The caterpillar's first three pairs of legs (the "true" legs) are jointed, and each has a little claw at the end. Farther down on its body are five pairs of prolegs, which it uses for gripping. The last pair, the anal prolegs, are separated from the others by a wide space.

The caterpillar's major function is to store energy for the rest of its life cycle. It therefore spends most of its time eating. When they are small, caterpillars prefer younger, tender leaves, but when caterpillars are mature, almost any part of the foodplant is fodder—even stems. A single caterpillar doesn't eat much of a plant, perhaps a small group of leaves. If you have a large plant, this doesn't make a dent. The combined effect

Anise Swallowtail caterpillar

of a great number of caterpillars can be pronounced, but predation and other environmental factors usually inhibit their activity and keep their effects within acceptable bounds.

Caterpillars have evolved some very effective methods of protecting themselves. Some feed at night, while day feeders commonly blend in well with their foodplants. The Cabbage White even adopts its food-plants' shades of green, from the rich green of nasturtium to the pale green of cabbage. Caterpillars often feed from the underside of the leaf, just exposing their heads along the edge where they're chewing. They tend to rest on the underside of leaves too, which keeps them out of sight of predators and shields them from the sun. Some caterpillars have spines or hairs that repel predators. Others, such as the Monarch, feed on poisonous plants—in its case, milkweed. These species assimilate the toxins of their hosts and become distasteful to potential predators. Swallowtail larvae project two-pronged, light-orange, fleshy organs called osmeteria from the top of their heads when provoked. The osmeteria emit a pungent odor that smells sweetish at first but quickly takes on a repulsive odor. The osmeteria are believed to repel predators with their sight and smell.

Monarch caterpillar

Like all insects, caterpillars have their skeleton on the outside—what you'd think of as their skin. This covering, the exoskeleton, is composed of a tough material called chitin. As the caterpillar eats, it grows—but the skin only stretches to a point. When the caterpillar gets too big for its skin, it forms a new skin underneath and eventually crawls out of the old skin, a process called molting. Then it resumes eating, and the new skin expands until it hardens. When the caterpillar outgrows this new skin, it molts again. Caterpillars usually molt four or five times before becoming chrysalises, and butterfly gardening will give you many opportunities to watch this process occur. But it only takes a few minutes so you have to watch closely in order to catch it. Watch for a telltale sign that it's going

Monarch chrysalis

Anise Swallowtail chrysalis

to happen soon: The caterpillar stops eating for about a day and remains where it is on the plant.

The change from a caterpillar to a chrysalis is sudden and complete. First, the fully grown caterpillar stops feeding and begins searching for a suitable place to pupate (i.e., turn into a chrysalis). It may take the better part of a day for a caterpillar to find a spot with which it is happy. Usually this will be a secluded or sheltered place, such as the eave of an old barn, the stem of a nearby plant, or a dead leaf on its foodplant, where it will blend in. The caterpillar spins a tiny pad of silk on the surface and hooks its anal prolegs into the silk pad. Then it molts again, but this time, instead of a larger caterpillar emerging, the chrysalis appears.

Different species of butterflies pupate in different ways and places. The Gulf Fritillary and its relatives in the Nymphalidae family hang in a "J" position from the silk pad for a number of hours before shedding their final larval skin. The chrysalis then hangs head-down. Swallowtails pupate head-up from the silken pad, and they spin a girdle of silk to hold themselves in place. In many species, the chrysalis takes only ten days or two weeks for the butterfly to emerge but since other species overwinter as pupae, it can take much longer.

During the pupal stage, phenomenal changes take place inside the chrysalis. First, the contents of the caterpillar are broken down into a viscous substance. Meanwhile, the cells of the butterfly are activated, and gradually the wings, head, thorax, and abdomen develop. You can start to see the tiny but developed wings within some pupae after four or five days. If you touch the chrysalis, it will gyrate. A chrysalis may ward off a wandering caterpillar (ready to pupate), or repel a potential predator, by repeatedly thrusting itself ninety degrees to each side of its vertical, upside down position.

Shortly before a butterfly emerges, the appearance of the chrysalis changes noticeably. The clear wing cases of the Cabbage White turn from green to white one day. You can even see the black patch on the corner of the forewing. A day or so before the Gulf Fritillary emerges, the chrysalis begins to turn from light brown to a dark, reddish brown. About twelve hours before emergence, this red sandstone color consumes the entire chrysalis. Perhaps no butterfly exhibits a more dramatic change in coloration just before emerging than the Monarch, which turns from jade green to orange and black, within some nine hours.

Most butterflies emerge in the morning so as to take advantage of the sunny day, which will enable them to fly forth and forage for nectar and search for mates. Immediately after emerging the butterfly's body is immense and swollen and the wings appear crumpled up and deformed. A few minutes later, having been pumped up and flattened out, the wings have assumed full size and the body has shrunk to its proper proportions. Next the butterfly holds its wings apart slightly to allow them to dry. It usually remains where it is for at least an hour before flying, and often longer. Some butterflies open and close their wings repeatedly, perhaps as a drying function.

Since it cannot yet fly, the period just after a butterfly emerges presents a marvelous opportunity to observe it closely. In perfect condition, the butterfly has not yet been ravaged by winds or scratched itself on leaves and branches. Its wings perfect, colors fresh, and every scale intact, a newly emerged butterfly glistens in its perfection.

Butterfly scales overlap like roof shingles and come in two types: pigmented scales produce brown, black, yellow, orange, white, and red; and structural scales, which refract light, produce metallic and iridescent hues of blue, silver, purple, violet, and green. The males of many species have sex scales called androconia on their wings. Distinguishable as small black patches (stigmata) or as narrow strips, androconia disperse pheromones, or scent hormones, that are produced by glands in the wings. The black patches on the Monarch male's hindwings are highly noticeable examples of androconia. It is easy to rub off a butterfly's scales. They leave a "powder" on your fingers. If rubbed enough, a butterfly's wings will be rendered transparent.

Ready to fly for the first time, a butterfly opens and closes its wings several times, as if warming them up. Then its body quivers slightly, and in a flash, it rises from its perch and flutters up into the air. The flight of a butterfly is a wonderful thing to see. It seems so effortless, as if the butterfly were weightless and carried away by the wind. Actually, each species has its own directed pattern of flight, which is not at all random.

Different butterflies fly in different ways, from the darting flight of the skippers to the lilting flight of the Monarch. The Cabbage White bobs along in an almost frenetic fashion, while the Gulf Fritillary resembles an orb as it sails smoothly by. The Gray Hairstreak zips up, down and around, like a fly, and Marine Blues flutter in small circles near their foodplant. Swallowtails glide across wide distances, flapping occasionally for acceleration, while the Painted Lady travels rapidly, in an almost direct line.

Butterflies usually will not fly unless the sun is out. This may be because they need the sun to warm them up, although some scientists believe orientation or storm protection may be more crucial. When it's in the low to mid-sixties and sunny, you'll see butterflies on the wing, but if it's cloudy, you probably won't, even when it gets into the seventies. When the sun is out and the temperature is in the seventies or eighties, you'll see plenty of butterflies. Since butterflies are sun-loving, you can almost predict the weather by watching them. If they're flying around happily one minute and suddenly disappear, dropping to the ground or

Western Tiger Swallowtail

Western Tiger Swallowtail

taking cover beneath a leaf, chances are pretty good that clouds will soon cover the area and a storm may impend.

Just as butterfly flight displays particular patterns, all aspects of butterfly behavior follow refined, instinctive lines. The poetic perception that butterflies simply waft away their lives in careless reverie is entirely false. Butterfly behavior has much more substance than that, and it offers one of the best reasons for watching them in your garden. Once the butterflies are on the wing, a butterfly garden will furnish many fine opportunities to observe their behavior. One of the first things you'll notice is that butterflies can fly very fast. If you try to run after them, you'll be hard-pressed to keep up. Of course, when butterflies drink nectar or lay eggs, they will hover, or alight.

Some butterflies, such as skippers and hairstreaks, establish territories that they defend by chasing away unwanted visitors. The Pearl Crescent has the reputation of being pugnacious, as it darts out from its perch after interlopers. Scientists are unsure as to whether these encounters are motivated by a defense of territory, as they are with vertebrates, or whether butterflies are simply investigating passing objects as possible females of the same species. There is no doubt, however, that butterflies do exhibit territorial behavior. I once flushed a Fiery Skipper repeatedly from its perch on an evergreen shrub near a lantana bush. Within moments, it always returned to the tip of the very same leaf from which it had been frightened away. Common Buckeyes and West Coast Ladies frequently come back to the same patch of bare ground, and Mourning Cloaks will reappear within minutes on the same high perch which they left.

Male butterflies either "perch" in one spot and fly out to investigate things, or they "patrol" an area by flying up and down a set route. Although they have little ability to damage each other, they sometimes get into full-scale battles. In his book *Near Horizons,* Edwin Way Teale describes the butterfly battles he observed in his own insect garden. One Red Admiral attacked him repeatedly as it defended its patch of sand. "Indeed," Teale recalls, "this particular butterfly appeared to have little fear in its makeup. On its swerving, swooping circuits of the hillside, it was ever on the alert for interlopers. It flew at a Monarch or a Yellow

Swallowtail far larger than itself, as quickly as at a Grayling [Common Wood Nymph] or a Painted Lady. . . . It attacked me as fearlessly as it did the smallest butterfly rival." Eventually, the Red Admiral accepted Teale and even rode along on his shirt or trousers. The last time he saw it, it was in heated aerial battle with a Mourning Cloak. The next day, the stretch of sand was empty. Teale never did find out what became of his interesting friend.

Once, on a damp trail, I was face-to-face with a Marine Blue for about twenty minutes. If I made a sudden movement, it flew off, but a few moments later, it would return to the spot in front of me. Occasionally, it sipped the water that had dampened the pebbles and ground. Finally, I continued down the trail. I probably could have stayed there and watched it all day. Many butterflies, usually males, are fond of sipping water from the damp sides of puddles and streams. Large groups of swallowtails, sulphurs, skippers, and blues often partake of this activity. Why do they form these "mud-puddle clubs"? One reason is for the moisture. But perhaps more important is to obtain the salts contained in the liquids. Indeed, it is not difficult to entice a butterfly to suck the perspiration on your finger, forehead, or nose. Try this when you see them puddling, as they will already be in the mood for what you have in mind. If you provide a puddle for the butterflies in your garden, you can watch this "puddling" to your heart's content.

One challenge is to try and find the roosting site of your garden's butterflies. Late in the afternoon, before the sun goes down, butterflies find a roosting spot for the night, but they're so good at camouflaging themselves that it is extremely difficult to find them. Butterflies usually roost in shrubs, trees, various plants with thick foliage, and grasses. Some butterflies roost on their foodplants. Species that stay close to their hosts, such as many members of the Lycaenidae family, may choose to roost there. Most butterflies roost singly, but Zebra Heliconians bed down communally, in groups of 25–30 individuals. In Florida, these aggregations can be observed as they gather at dusk, or they can be seen at night by flashlight.

Perhaps the best way to locate a butterfly's roosting spot is to observe it late in the day. One summer afternoon at about four, I watched a

Gulf Fritillary find a roosting spot on a drooping melaleuca. The butterfly perched in the shadows, next to some bare branches, and folded its wings. Only a few feet away, it looked like one of the twigs. From ten or fifteen feet, it was virutally impossible to distinguish it from its surroundings. This camouflage protects butterflies from predators during a very vulnerable period.

Indeed, life for butterflies is anything but safe. They must always be on their guard against predators—be they spiders and wasps, which capture caterpillars, pupae, and adults; ants, which prey on eggs; dragonflies, which pick adults out of the sky and devour them; or birds, which feed on caterpillars and also eat adults, spitting out the wings.

More butterflies probably lose their lives to parasitoids than predators. Many species of flies and wasps attack butterfly eggs, caterpillars, and pupae. Braconid wasps, for instance, lay their eggs in the young caterpillar; later, the tiny wasp larvae bore their way out of the caterpillar's body, on which they have been feeding, and spin tiny, straw-colored cocoons right next to or on it. The mortally wounded caterpillar dies shortly thereafter. Chalcid wasps lay their eggs directly in the newly formed chrysalis, boring through the soft case with their ovipositor. The eggs hatch and the wasp larvae feed on the chrysalis, killing it. Later the wasps fly out of the pupal case, leaving the tiny hole from which they've escaped.

Butterflies have adopted many methods of protection from their predators. Some butterflies possess targets that divert bird attacks away from the head and body. The Common Buckeye, for instance, has three large, bluish-purple eyespots along the edges of its wings. Many satyrs have similar eyespots. Hairstreaks sport tails and bright spots, or false heads, on the undersides of their hindwings. When at rest, they rub their hindwings back and forth, drawing attention to them. Most blues don't have tails, but many have similar spots on their hindwings. They, too, rub them together. The tails of swallowtails serve a similar function, with red spots to further advertise their presence. It is not uncommon to see butterflies such as these with a piece of their wing or a tail torn away by a bird.

Remarkably effective use of camouflage may be seen in rough-edged butterflies such as the Eastern Comma, the Satyr Comma, and the

Common Buckeye

closely related Mourning Cloak. The brown or gray, mottled undersides of these butterflies blend in so well with tree trunks that the butterflies become almost impossible to see. Furthermore, their jagged wings make them look like old, tattered leaves. Some of these butterflies even drop to the ground and play dead, blending in with the leaves. Many of these species possess bright-orange uppersides, the sudden flashing of which will startle a bird momentarily and give the butterfly a chance to escape. When these butterflies are on the wing their bright colors show, but when they land they expose their ventral surfaces only and in an instant become virtually invisible.

Coloration can also draw attention to a butterfly. The unpalatable Monarch makes birds regurgitate should they attempt to eat one of these butterflies. Thus, the bright orange and black coloring of the Monarch's wings serves as a warning. Birds learn this pattern and avoid further encounters. The Viceroy, like many butterflies, has evolved coloration that mimics a toxic model species. Almost a twin to the Monarch, it is perfectly edible because its foodplants aren't poisonous. But birds that have learned to avoid the Monarch also avoid the Viceroy. Thus, the

Viceroy

Viceroy's coloration contributes importantly to its survival. Evolution has brought about butterfly colors in ways such as these.

Anyone who has spent time in an alfalfa field has seen Orange and Clouded Sulphurs circling high overhead. This signals the early stage of butterfly courtship, one of the most fascinating aspects of butterfly behavior. Aggressive males will buzz females, fly up into the air with them if they prove receptive, and then follow them down to a perch. Here, a courtship "dance" ensues. These minuets often involve distinctive steps that allow members of the same species to recognize each other and thus avoid crossbreeding. During this courtship dance, the male and female often circle each other and touch their antennae to the other's wings. Females sense male pheromones with their antennae, either in the air or by brushing up against the androconia on the wings, and this makes them more receptive to mating. Sometimes males hover over females and even bombard them repeatedly. If the female is ready to mate, the male positions himself behind her and connects his abdomen to hers. Butterflies always mate back-to-back. Mating lasts from twenty minutes to as long as two hours, sometimes overnight. The pair will even fly around and feed while they're connected, and they'll move if they're disturbed. In this case, the heavier, stronger female usually carries the male. An already-mated or unreceptive female tells interested males that she's not available by fluttering or buzzing her wings rapidly, or by raising her abdomen toward the sky.

It's easy to see a female laying her eggs. If you wish to observe this, follow a female as she goes about her business, taking care not to disturb her. Eventually she may alight on a foodplant and commence oviposition. If she's going to lay eggs, she'll hover over the plant or perch and crawl around on it, deliberately moving from stem to stem, checking out the leaves.

The intricate behavior of butterflies may best be appreciated up close. Unlike birds, butterflies will allow you to get up to within inches of them, and they won't fly away. They may be busy nectaring, puddling, or simply perched on a leaf. No matter. They may be approached closely in many attitudes—but only if you take great care, because rapid movements will frighten them away. Unless they're really preoccupied, you must be slow, quiet, and stealthy. It is all right to touch butterflies gently, but be careful not to injure them. The best way to approach a butterfly is from the side or below. If you approach them from above, chances are they will fly off. That's because of their natural awareness of predators, many of which attack them from above.

Once you're close to butterflies, you'll be amazed at how humanlike their behavior appears. One day, I saw a Monarch holding itself on a narrow twig by the tips of its front legs, much as a human would rest his left hand on his right hand. A butterfly will turn its head from side to side, in short, rapid motions, and will tilt its palpi out briefly from time to time, as if yawning. When a butterfly is sipping nectar from a flower head, you can watch its extended proboscis probe flower after flower. All of these actions have their reasons that have to do with survival and maintenance.

If you were standing across the street from a butterfly, it might appear as an object that flitters by, stops, and then takes off. But looking at it up close makes you realize that butterflies are more than just pretty objects fluttering around, with no apparent purpose. The more you observe and learn about butterflies, the more successful you'll be at providing for them. By appreciating their biology and behavior, you will be able to anticipate their needs. In addition to offering them the necessary food-plants and nectar sources, you may want to furnish special sites for pupation, hibernation, basking, and puddling. Every aspect of the creature's life history and activity may be incorporated into your butterfly garden design, if you first come to understand the details of butterfly lives. By understanding what butterflies are all about, you will understand what is going on in your butterfly garden. This will enable you to enjoy it to the fullest.

Gulf Fritillary

CHAPTER 3
Regions and Seasons

In Canada, the Memorial University of Newfoundland Botanical Garden provides larval foodplants and nectar sources especially for local butterflies. Original curator Bernard Jackson reported that of the 48 butterfly species that occur on the island, 26 had been sighted in the garden. Along with wide-ranging species like the Monarch, Cabbage White, and Painted Lady, the garden attracts regional or primarily northern species such as the Short-tailed Swallowtail, Pink-edged Sulphur, Common Ringlet, Jutta Arctic, Northern Blue, and Arctic Skipper. None of these latter species occur in Southern California. Here, butterfly gardeners seek to attract regional and local species such as the West Coast Lady, Acmon Blue, and California Dogface, in addition to widespread species like the Common Buckeye and Gray Hairstreak.

In Seattle, butterfly gardeners select from a number of butterfly species that are common in the Pacific Northwest. Few of these occur in Southern California or Newfoundland. These include the Clodius Parnassian, "Margined" Mustard White, "Ochre" Common Ringlet, and Woodland Skipper. The butterfly garden at the Neale Woods Nature Center in Omaha attracts a number of butterfly species that are known for their occurrence in the prairie states—including the Regal Fritillary, Tawny Emperor, Northern Pearly-eye, and Silvery Checkerspot.

All these examples demonstrate the regionality of butterflies. Many factors govern the ranges of butterflies. Whereas generalists such as the Monarch, Orange Sulphur, and Cabbage White are found nearly everywhere, the Eastern Comma exists primarily in the East; the Sara Orangetip in the West; and the Queen in the South. The most common

Cabbage White

Queen

butterflies in your area may not be the most widespread species, and may be quite rare or altogether absent a short distance away. It behooves you to keep your antennae out for these species, since they should do well in your butterfly garden.

The distribution of butterflies may be described in large part by biogeographic "life zones," each of which has its own distinctive flora and fauna. Latitude and altitude help to determine which life zone will occur in a given area. The Tropical Life Zone (average midsummer temperature of 80°F and above) occurs in the southernmost parts of Florida, Texas, Arizona, and California; the Lower Austral (78.8°F and above) in the Deep South and southern portions of the Southwest; the Upper Austral (71.6-78.8°F) in a diagonal strip from New Jersey to northern Georgia, across the central part of the country roughly between 40 and 43 degrees latitude, in the Great Basin, and parts of the Southwest; the Transition (64.4-71.6°F) in the northern part of the United States and Appalachia; the Canadian (57.2-64.4°F) in a horizontal strip across central Canada and in mountain areas of the Northeast, Appalachians, Rockies, and Sierra Nevada; the Hudsonian (50-57.2°F) across northern Canada and high on mountainsides in the northeastern United States and Rockies; and the Arctic-Alpine (42.8-50°F) in the Far North and above the tree line on high mountain peaks.

Within each of these life zones, temperature and rainfall are the two most important environmental factors determining where butterflies exist and when they'll be on the wing. Temperature is determined primarily by latitude and altitude, as well as distance from the sea. In the warmer southern United States, butterflies remain on the wing for a longer period during the year than in the North. The higher the latitude, the colder the weather, and the shorter the flying season. Increased altitude causes the same effect. All butterflies have their limits of tolerance of heat and cold, but most species range over a number of different regions.

Nevertheless, some butterflies exist primarily within a given life zone. For instance, the Polydamas Swallowtail, Zebra Heliconian, and Julia Heliconian occur in the Tropical; the Palamedes Swallowtail, Gulf Fritillary, and Southern Pearly-eye in the Lower Austral; the Regal Fritillary,

Polydamas Swallowtail

Zebra Heliconian

Diana Fritillary, and Eyed Brown in the Upper Austral; the Baltimore Checkerspot, Weidemeyer's Admiral, and Silver-bordered Fritillary in the Transition; the Green Comma, Hoary Comma, and Atlantis Fritillary in the Canadian; the Old World Swallowtail and Cranberry Blue in the Hudsonian; and the Melissa Arctic and Sierra Sulphur in the Arctic–Alpine.

Rainfall, along with temperature, determines which plants may grow in an area, and hence which butterflies can exist there. A caterpillar that feeds on a plant native to the southwestern desert might not find suitable food in a rainier region, and would therefore not be found there. The converse is also true. Generally, few butterflies occur in areas of extreme dryness or rainfall, whereas many occur in the regions in between.

In addition to the temperature and rainfall, habitat type helps determine the distribution of butterflies. Anglewings, for instance, like forest edges, roads, and glades. Some fritillaries prefer prairies, others mountain meadows. The Palamedes Swallowtail and Baltimore Checkerspot occupy swamps and wet meadows respectively. Many skippers, and satyrs such as the Common Wood-Nymph, prefer grassy areas, because grasses

Palamedes Swallowtail

Common Wood-Nymph

are their foodplants. Some butterflies thrive in areas that have been altered by man but in which butterfly foodplants and nectar sources continue to grow. These habitats include abandoned railway lines, vacant lots, roadsides, agricultural fields, and gardens. The Orange Sulphur, for example, proliferates in alfalfa fields. Many of the butterflies in our "Fifty North American Garden Butterflies" section thrive in just such areas, as well as in wild habitats.

Historically, physical corridors and barriers have accounted for butterflies' ability to get from place to place. For example, riverbanks serve as butterfly highways, enabling wandering species to extend their range. Thick forests, arid basins, and industrial zones may prevent butterfly movement, restricting their range.

Because of all these factors, each region of the country has a special combination of plants and butterflies. In the tropical scrub areas associated with the hardwood hammocks in southern Florida, Atala larvae feed on cycads and the Ruddy Daggerwing utilizes figs. In the moist maple and beech forests of the Northeast, the Appalachians, and the northern Midwest, the Gray Comma feeds on wild gooseberry. In the northern deciduous and mixed coniferous forests, the Compton Tor-toiseshell and White Admiral feed on birches, willows, and poplars; while in western desert canyons and washes, the "Desert" Black Swallowtail feeds on turpentine broom in the Southwest and the "Oregon" Swallowtail on dragon wormwood in the Northwest. The acid bogs of the northern Midwest and New England host the Bog Copper on cranberries; in southern swamps, the Creole Pearly-eye frequents canebrakes; and in the tallgrass prairies of the central region, the Dakota Skipper and Poweshiek Skipperling are threatened by the destruction of their grasslands. Southern pine flats have Georgia Satyrs among grasses and Little Metalmarks around yellow thistle; and in northern and southern broad-leaf deciduous forests, the Red-spotted Purple and Eastern Tiger Swallowtail haunt wild cherry, poplar, aspen, and other broad-leaved trees.

Butterflies react to seasonal as well as regional factors. They have their own built-in time clocks that determine when during the year they'll hatch and mate, and how far they'll range. Life cycles, however, can depend greatly on environmental conditions. Each generation of butterflies is called a brood. In the northern and central part of the country, most species have one or two broods, a few three. In the Sun Belt, the majority of butterflies have three broods and some have four. In the extreme South, most species breed four or five times and can be seen almost year-round. Some species single-brooded in the North will have two or more broods farther south. Obviously, the number of generations possible in a given location has tremendous implications for the butterfly garden.

The more broods a species has, the longer we can see it on the wing. However, some butterflies with fewer broods live longer than those with more and we can observe them for many months of the year. The migratory fall generation of the Monarch lives six to eight months, while hibernators such as the Mourning Cloak and Eastern Comma may live nine months or more. On the other hand, adult Spring Azures live for only a few days.

As a rule, butterflies live anywhere from one to three weeks after emerging and seldom more than a month. Many species with overlapping broods are visible throughout the summer, but some single-generation species, such as certain blues and browns, appear for just a few days or weeks each year. It may be more challenging, though at times frustrating, to try to attract such limited species. Butterflies that take flight in early spring include the Checkered White, Sara and Falcate Orangetips, Silvery Blue, Satyr Comma, Common Buckeye, and the aptly named Spring Azure. Species that begin flying in late spring or in summer include the Giant Swallowtail, Southern Dogface, Great Spangled Fritillary, American Lady, and White Admiral. Late summer and fall see the flight of butterflies such as the Pine White, overwintering generations of anglewings and tortoiseshells, skippers such as the Leonard's Skipper, and the autumn generation of the Monarch. The farther south you get, the earlier the spring butterflies will emerge, and the later the butterflies will disappear in the fall.

Butterflies pass the winter in a variety of ways. Most species hibernate in either the egg, caterpillar, or chrysalis stage. The young caterpillars of the Viceroy, White Admiral, and Red-spotted Purple construct a hibernaculum in the fall by rolling up a leaf of the foodplant into a tube and securing it with silk, having attached the leaf to the twig with silk so that it doesn't fall off with the rest of the leaves. In the spring they leave

Giant Swallowtail

Southern Dogface

their shelters and begin to feed on the new growth. If you have willows in your garden, you can inspect them for hibernaculi in the winter, then see the young caterpillars resume feeding when the fresh leaves begin to unfurl.

Species that overwinter as chrysalises include most swallowtails, whites, and blues. Many fritillaries, checkerspots, browns, and others overwinter as caterpillars. Some butterflies, such as the anglewings and tortoiseshells, overwinter as adults and hibernate in hollow trees, cracks in walls, and open barns. It is a curious but lovely sight on a mild January day, with snow still on the ground, to see a Mourning Cloak flittering through the air, awakened by the warmth. It retreats into hibernation as the day cools.

Some butterflies extend their range northward temporarily, usually during the summer months. When the weather turns cold, these butterflies usually die off. Though not annual migrators like the Monarch, they may sometimes be seen in great swarms. The Painted Lady is especially noted for this, as it recolonizes the North and the East from Mexico and the Southwest every year. When conditions favor reproduction, the numbers involved may be immense; other years they remain scarce. The Common

Painted Lady

Cloudless Sulphur

Great Southern White

Buckeye, American Lady, and Red Admiral also emigrate periodically. Some southern butterflies, because their populations become so great, emigrate north but then die off when the weather gets cold. These include the Gulf Fritillary, Dainty Sulphur, Cloudless Sulphur, Variegated Fritillary, Reakirt's Blue, Long-tailed Skipper, and Great Southern White. None of these southern immigrants to the north possess the ability to withstand cold winters, so they must recolonize the temperate states annually.

Not all species move about in this fashion. Butterfly mobility varies a great deal. Some tiny butterflies, such as the Western Pygmy-Blue are nomadic, while some large butterflies, including the Zebra Swallowtail, are stay-at-home species. Characteristics like these are determined by the genetic makeup of each species.

Only one butterfly possesses true, birdlike migration. In September and early October, you may be able to see great swarms of migrating Monarchs on their way to their winter destinations. From New England, the Eastern Seaboard, and the Midwest, they move in a southerly direction, flying over city and country alike on their 2,000–3,000 mile journey. Cutting over to the Gulf Coast and moving south through

Texas, the eastern and central Monarchs travel high into the mountains of central Mexico, where they pass the winter clinging to tall fir trees and occasionally flying down for nectar and water. The western and Sierra Nevada Monarchs migrate to the central and southern coast of California, where they overwinter at a number of dispersed sites. The most famous of these sites is in Pacific Grove, a town on the Monterey Peninsula, where thousands of Monarchs spend the winter roosting in a grove of Monterey pine, cypress, and eucalyptus trees.

In early March, the butterflies become active, mate, and begin their journey east and north. Along the way, females lay their eggs on milkweed plants. Several summer generations ensue, the number depending upon altitude and latitude. In the fall, the last of the summer generations repeats the great migration. How they do it, without the benefit of parental teaching, remains one of the great mysteries of instinct.

If you have a butterfly garden along the route of these migrating Monarchs, it may serve as a valuable refueling station and breeding ground. This lets you assist in the remarkable phenomenon. But wherever you are, you should be able to suit your garden to some butterflies, including regional specialties such as the Clodius Parnassian in the Northwest or the Jutta Arctic in the Northeast. Perhaps you'll share your garden with the Giant Swallowtail in the South; the Regal Fritillary in the prairie states; or the Marine Blue in the Southwest. Wherever you are, some butterflies will find your garden. Then it's up to you to make it ready for them.

Gulf Fritillary

Cabbage White

CHAPTER 4

Getting Started

In his book *Create a Butterfly Garden,* L. Hugh Newman describes his own butterfly garden in Kent, England. On a sunny, south-facing, terraced hillside, Newman allows wildflowers, grasses, and a large nettlebed to grow uncut until autumn. These provide a steady supply of nectar sources and larval foodplants for a rich variety of British butterflies. Cultivated flowers complement the wild plants. No insecticides are used, and hedges and bushes furnish shelter. Shady as well as sunny spots abound, since different butterflies prefer each. "I have, over a number of years," Newman states, "deliberately tried to produce conditions that butterflies like."

The butterfly garden at the Drum Manor Forest Park in Northern Ireland was built in a walled garden of an old estate turned public park. Henry George Heal, then of Queen's University of Belfast, wrote that the garden exists in a windy, maritime region with low summer air temperatures and limited hours of sunshine many months of the year. The wall, erected to protect vegetables, now shelters butterflies. Tall trees on the northeast and northwest sides of the wall provide further protection. "There are many hazy days in summer when it takes the shelter of a south-facing wall or wood border to tempt most butterflies into activity," Heal reported.

These two gardens illustrate perhaps the most important principle of butterfly gardening—provide the environment butterflies need for survival. This includes not only nectar sources and larval foodplants but other essential ingredients such as adequate sunlight, shelter, and water. The more you re-create the natural habitats of butterflies, whether meadows, grasslands, or forest, the better chance you'll have to attract and convince them to stay.

But while certain principles should be followed in order to ensure your best success, butterfly gardening rewards creativity and imagination, and invites you to add your own personal touch. Plenty of different plants may be selected and arranged in a wide variety of designs. Nectar sources and foodplants include grasses, annuals and perennials, herbs, shrubs, trees, vines, even vegetables—and you can garden with cultivated plants as well as native species.

But where to begin? First, you must determine which butterflies and plants you want. Looking around your neighborhood will help you decide. Do some fieldwork in wild areas, botanical gardens, your neighbors' yards, and your own place. By surveying local butterflies and the plants they visit, you will develop realistic expectations and an idea of the easiest butterflies to attract.

Don't be shy about contacting experts at your local natural history museum or university. If you are fortunate enough to have a local entomology club, members who have been observing butterflies in your area for years will no doubt be delighted to share their knowledge. The more information you have before you start your butterfly garden, the better off you'll be.

Many factors will determine the type of butterfly garden you'll have. The location of your garden plays a critical role. Latitude, altitude, exposure, rainfall, shade, atmospheric, and soil conditions vary from place to place. The proximity of your garden to urban or rural areas will also affect the number and variety of butterflies you may expect to attract. For instance, the Gulf Fritillary feeds on passion flower in many southern cities, and the West Coast Lady thrives on cheeseweed in urban vacant lots. But the Diana Fritillary lives in Appalachian forests with streams, and the Olympia Marble inhabits such places as shale barrens, river bluffs, and rocky foothills. If your garden is in one of these settings, and within the range of these butterflies, you might be able to attract them. Constraints such as these will determine the complexion of your garden. But they also provide an opportunity for enterprising butterfly lovers to exploit the flora and fauna of their regions and create their own distinctive butterfly gardens.

Butterfly gardeners should only attract butterflies that occur naturally in the region in which their butterfly garden exists. And a butterfly should never be introduced to a garden unless it could otherwise fly there on its own. There are many reasons why butterflies (and other insects) should not be transported outside of their natural ranges. In the absence of natural enemies, they may become pests. The Cabbage White, since its introduction to Quebec from Europe in 1860, has aggravated farmers and gardeners by becoming a pest on crucifers. The introduction of exotic species can also damage the gene pools of native fauna and disrupt the biogeographical records of scientists. As with weeds, introduced insects in the absence of natural enemies may run rampant and crowd out native species. Furthermore, non-native insects could spread diseases and parasites that can affect endemic flora and fauna.

Once you've made a thorough local survey and decided which butterflies and plants you want, then you must design your garden to best suit them. Here, a number of guidelines come into play. Since butterflies are sun-loving creatures, they should be provided with a large, open area filled with sunlight. Most butterfly gardeners prefer placing this sunny region in the center of the garden, but you can create open areas in corners of the garden as well. This open area may be planted with grasses, with ground cover such as clover and alfalfa, or with other low-growing host or nectar plants. Nectar sources and foodplants should be in the sun and should not be heavily shaded by trees or buildings. Create sun traps, and employ southern exposures to get the most sun during the day.

Butterflies need adequate shelter from the wind, so it's a good idea to design a butterfly garden within the confines of a wall or a windbreak of shrubs or trees. The garden doesn't have to be completely surrounded. One side of the house and a row of shrubs will do. However, the more protection you provide, the better off your butterflies will be. Shrubby nectar sources such as butterfly bush, honeysuckle, and New Jersey tea will do this job nicely, as well as foodplants like spicebush, hawthorn, and hibiscus. Trees that serve as foodplants, such as willow, poplar, and wild cherry, offer more options for shelter. Vines including hops, pipevine, and passion flower can be run up trellises or along walls or fences, to function as windscreens as well as larval hosts.

Somewhere in your open area, a puddle should be provided. In fact, you might want to create a number of puddles throughout the garden, with perhaps a big one in the center. You can grade your garden to produce moist areas by creating an incline with a sandy basin at the bottom. When it rains, the water will flow into the basin and keep it moist. Or hose it down until it's wet, but don't leave standing water on the surface. Butterflies cannot drink from open water. The "puddles" they use in nature are really damp sand, earth, and mud, at the edge of pools, streams, or seeps.

In order to create a homemade "puddle," you can bury a bowl in the ground and fill the bowl with sand or gravel. Put a few rocks and sticks on the sand and fill the bowl with water. Butterflies will drink from the puddle and from the moisture around the edge of the bowl. Place the bowl in an open area, perhaps along a path. You could add stale beer, sugar water, or fruit to the bowl, in order to attract the butterflies.

Since butterflies love to bask in the sun, every butterfly garden should have a rock garden or patio where butterflies can soak up the warmth of the sun and the rocks. Nectar sources such as sedum, aubrietia, and primrose are well suited for rock gardens. Situated on terraces, they may serve to shelter the central part of the garden. Puddles and basking spots go well together, since butterflies like to alternate the two activities. Basking spots encourage butterflies to appear on hazy days when flight might otherwise be postponed.

The meadow habitat is perhaps the most popular butterfly environment, and butterfly gardens should have one or more of these. In meadows, butterflies hide and lay eggs in tall grasses and herbs; nectar and oviposit on wildflowers; and generally fly around in a bed of riches. In order to create a flowering meadow in her butterfly garden, one Northeastern butterfly gardener sowed meadow grasses, scattered wildflower seeds, and planted patches of native plants. Soon, daisies, wild asters, yarrow, and many other wildflowers began to grow.

Miriam Rothschild, co-author of *The Butterfly Gardener*, had an acre of meadow in her butterfly garden at Ashton, England. Here, meadow grasses and wildflowers such as field scabious, knapweeds, and thistles supported resident colonies of the Meadow Brown, Wall, Gatekeeper, Small Skipper, Common Blue, and other British butterflies. Rothschild was particularly enamored of her "hayfield," as she called it. "On warm evenings," she writes, "I walk through it after dark and imagine it stretches away for thirty acres or more on all sides." She adds that small meadow areas could be created under trees or in borders along lawns, but that they probably would not be large enough to support breeding colonies of grass feeders like the first four species mentioned above.

In addition to meadows, butterfly gardeners might want to create other mini-environments in their gardens. For instance, a wooded area will entice satyrs and Mourning Cloaks, which enjoy gliding through sunny glades in otherwise shady areas; and a patch of bare ground will attract Common Buckeyes and Red-spotted Purples, which love to sun themselves on open trails. If you place a stump in your wood, you can sit and watch the butterflies glide by. And if you put a table with an umbrella or a bench with a canopy next to a glade, you'll have a good observation post from which to observe the festivities.

One butterfly gardener I visited was in the process of building a large mound of dirt in the center of his garden, to simulate the mountainous habitat of a number of butterflies. He planned to place large rocks in various spots on the "mountain," and create other nooks and crannies, so the butterflies could find shelter from excessive heat or cold. Using imaginative techniques like this will increase your chances of attracting the butterflies you want.

Planning out the color schemes of butterflies and flowers also gives you a chance to let your imagination run free. For instance, an Eastern Tiger Swallowtail nectaring on a purple butterfly bush makes a beautiful color combination; an orange and black Monarch on a goldenrod looks harmonious; and a Great Southern White on an orange lantana strikes the eye pleasingly. Actually, few colors clash in nature; but with so many elements available, why not suit your own tastes?

Once you've decided which butterflies and plants you want, you have to decide where in your garden you're going to put the plants. It's a good idea to place taller plants in the rear, medium-sized plants in the middle, and lower flowers in the front row of the garden. This allows you to see all the flowers and the activity around them, and it also contributes to the sheltered aspect of the garden.

Perennial and annual borders, when placed in front of a stone wall or wood fence, create sheltered areas where butterflies can bask. While the colors of perennials are constant, annuals offer the option of change. Long-blooming annuals such as marigolds, zinnias, and impatiens provide large splashes of the same or different colors in beds or borders. Annuals planted in the same border as perennials complement their long-lived neighbors. Borders such as these soften the edges of fences, houses, paths, and lawns. They also enable you to leave the central part of the garden open, so butterflies can fly freely and survey their surroundings.

Large flower beds take up a lot of space and do not suit some gardens. But a number of small beds placed throughout the garden will create oases for butterflies, without dominating the landscape. Of course, nothing's to stop you from planting a large bed in the middle of your butterfly garden. You might create a one-ring circus that will provide you with long hours of amusement, watching butterflies do their tricks.

One Southern California butterfly gardener that I visited used baby's tears, a foodplant of the Red Admiral, as a ground cover in his flower border. The plant's pale-green color complemented the bright green of his adjacent lawn. Ground cover such as sweet alyssum and ageratum, both excellent nectar sources, make pleasing expanses in borders or as edgings. You can also plant foodplants along a path or driveway, since butterflies like to fly along pathways. Planting a row of trees or bushes on either side of an open area will create the same effect. Not wishing to fight the obstacles, butterflies will fly down the center of the path. Nectar sources and larval foodplants placed between these boundaries will further entice the butterflies to stay.

Butterfly gardening usually involves combining formal and more natural gardening. Formal gardens and lawn areas are often placed next to houses, while patches of wildflowers and tall grasses can flourish in corners of the garden or along special rows. Butterflies should find these natural areas attractive. You can make them as large or as small as you want. By letting your flowers grow naturally, you won't have to work as hard to maintain the garden. This will give you more time to relax and enjoy it.

Gardening with wildflowers presents its own set of circumstances. Some wildflowers establish themselves in gardens with the help of the wind-carried seed. Others resist even the most painstaking care. If you select wildflowers that grow well in your region, you should have a chance at getting them to grow in your garden. Most wildflowers have the best chance of growing if they're started from seed. Later, you can collect the seeds they produce and scatter them throughout your garden.

Since butterfly gardening is a dynamic process, you should be on the constant lookout for plants that work well. A native plant might establish itself in your garden and become a prime nectar source or foodplant. Find out what it is and get more of it. You may discover that a butterfly uses a foodplant not previously recorded, or prefers one that isn't the favorite for that species. Always experiment. See which foodplants certain butterflies prefer; which locations suit the ovipositing females; which nectar sources work best for particular species and whether certain butterflies can be enticed to feed on things like rotting fruit or fermented beer. The Eastern Comma, Question Mark, Hackberry Emperor, and Red-spotted Purple are renowned for feeding on such items, and others may be similarly enticed.

Maintenance is an important aspect of butterfly gardening. When cutting back plants, be careful that caterpillars are not on them. If you have a meadow, mow it after the butterfly season is over. Miriam Rothschild cut her grass as soon as there were no more flowers in the hayfield, usually during the first two weeks of September. She waited a few days before removing the cut grass, enabling caterpillars to crawl down into the remains of their foodplants. Then she spread the cuttings in a nearby field, dispersing the seeds. When she had time, she separated the seed from the cut grass. She always left one section of her large garden uncut, "for the sake of larval butterflies." You could also mow half of a meadow one year and half the next, so as to allow butterflies, in various stages of development, to overwinter successfully.

As stated earlier, insecticides and herbicides should never be used in a butterfly garden. You can pick off unwanted insects or use soapy water on them. Biological controls, such as ladybugs for scale insects and aphids, provide effective protection against pests. By not killing off the insects in your garden, predators of all kinds will flourish enough to help control unwanted visitors.

If you have too many caterpillars on a foodplant, pick them off and give them to friends and neighbors. And if, for example, you have too many Black Swallowtail caterpillars on your parsley, you can pick them off and move them to a wild plant in the same family, such as Queen Anne's lace, which you have placed nearby, or transfer them to a foodplant in the wild, outside your garden. If you provide protective covering for eggs, caterpillars, and pupae, you can greatly reduce the number that fall prey to birds and other predators.

Most nectar sources and larval foodplants are available from standard nurseries, mail-order seed and plant suppliers, and, in the case of wildflowers, from native plant nurseries and seed companies. Botanical gardens often have comprehensive supplies of native plants and seeds for the region in which they're located. With a little bit of research you should be able to locate most of the plants you desire. Some rarer species may be a bit difficult to find. Botanical clubs and native plant societies may supply the information you need about particular plants. Authorities at botanical gardens, museums, and universities should also be happy to provide assistance.

Once you've decided which butterflies and plants you want for your butterfly garden, and you've made a general design with the butterflies' and plants' needs in mind, as well as your own aesthetic criteria, you'll have an opportunity to explore the possibilities of your garden in more detail. In the next two chapters, we'll discuss specific ways in which you can design and care for your nectar sources and larval foodplants.

Common Buckeye

Zebra Heliconian (foreground) and White Peacock (background)

CHAPTER 5

Nectar Sources

In 1950, a team of biologists from the New York Zoological Society, under the direction of William Beebe, began studying butterflies at a jungle field station in Trinidad. Seven years later, Jocelyn Crane, a scientist in the society's Department of Tropical Research, reported in *National Geographic* that butterflies in large cages at the field station were still providing scientists with opportunities to study such topics as insect evolution and courtship. The researchers also discovered something else—butterflies can be very finicky eaters. "They are as particular about their food as a spoiled child getting over the measles," Crane states. "The morphos, for instance, would much rather eat rotten bananas than sip the sweetest nectar. The heliconiids prefer a diet of nectar from lantana plants. . . . Little by little we discovered the preferred foods of our more finicky guests. They don't like much variety; each kind goes to its own few favorites, day after day, like a small girl who always orders chocolate sodas while her best friend sticks to vanilla malts."

Indeed, many butterflies prefer certain nectar sources. The determining factor may lie in nectar chemistry, or in the color, shape, or fragrance of the flowers. In addition, many nectar sources attract a wide variety of butterflies. By providing a combination of both types, you will attract the greatest variety and number of butterflies to your garden.

Most butterfly nectar sources have tubelike flowers arranged on a flower head, as with daisies, or in a cluster, as with butterfly bush. Since butterflies need a platform on which to land, they seldom use flowers that hang down, such as cardinal flower, which is used by hummingbirds. Neither do they use "double" ornamental blossoms and such flowers as hybrid ornamental roses and hydrangea, which usually possess no nectaries.

Pipevine Swallowtail (foreground) and Monarch (background)

White Peacock

Most experts believe that a flower's color attracts butterflies initially, since butterflies can detect color at a distance. Some butterflies see certain colors better than others. Gary Bernard, then at Yale University, discovered that nine out of seventeen butterfly species he studied had a spectral sensitivity in the longest red wavelengths. These included the Question Mark, Sleepy Orange, Cloudless Sulphur, and Eastern Tailed-Blue. This sensitivity was not found in the other species, which included the Hackberry Emperor, Mourning Cloak, and Common Buckeye.

On the other end of the visual spectrum, butterflies respond to ultra-violet light, which is invisible to man. Bernard states that this wide range of spectral sensitivity in butterflies represents "the broadest known of any animal." At Cornell University, Thomas Eisner and others used a television camera with an ultraviolet-transmitting lens to produce photographs of flowers as seen by man and by butterflies. The marsh marigold, which appears uniformly yellow to man, has large dark centers in the ultraviolet, which serve as nectar guides for butterflies and other insect pollinators, such as bees. Eisner photographed a group of five composites that look similar to us, but have differently sized dark patches in the ultraviolet, making them distinguishable to insects. He also photographed ultraviolet markings on butterflies, which highlight sexual dimorphism and serve as communication aids, as in mating. Birds and bats, which, unlike insects, have powerful long-range vision, pollinate flowers that lack ultraviolet nectar guides.

As stated in Chapter One, butterflies are attracted to a wide range of flower colors, including purple, blue, pink, yellow, orange, red, white, and shades in between. The color preferences of the Zebra Heliconian were studied by C. A. Swihart and S. L. Swihart. The Swiharts placed nine differently colored model flowers, each with a small sponge soaked in a solution of honey and B vitamins, on the ends of 0.4-meter-long wires. They fed the butterflies on these model flowers during the day, but removed the flowers from the cage in the evening. Each morning they randomly altered an arrangement of model flowers of the same colors, but which had not been in contact with the honey solution. For an hour each day, the feeding attempts of the butterflies were recorded—a feeding attempt defined as the butterfly alighting on the model and

Gulf Fritillary

Julia Heliconian

probing with its proboscis. The "spontaneous feeding preferences" of these butterflies included visits to all colors, but with peaks in the orange, red, blue-green, and blue regions of the spectrum.

In another series of experiments, the Swiharts fed the butterflies on nine yellow model flowers for two days before observing their feeding preferences on the test flowers, as used in previous experiments. The percentage of visits to yellow test models rose from 9.1 percent with the unconditioned butterflies to 49.6 percent with the conditioned ones. The Swiharts did a similar experiment with green flowers, which are extremely rare and are not considered instinctively attractive to butterflies. The percentage of visits to green flowers increased from 2 percent to 55.3 percent. In all of these experiments, the butterflies retained the searching image of their preferred flowers for approximately 15 hours, from the end of feeding one day until the start of testing the next, most of which time they were asleep.

Butterflies, therefore, clearly distinguish between different colors, and use color preferences when selecting the flowers they visit for nectar. But in order to get a drink, a butterfly must be able to reach the nectar. So the length of a butterfly's proboscis compared with the length of the flower tube of a nectar source determines in large part which flowers each butterfly will visit. The proboscis of most butterflies is about twice the length of the flower tubes they visit. Usually, butterflies with short proboscises visit short-tubed flowers, and those with long proboscises visit long-tubed flowers. In general, the larger the butterfly, the longer the proboscis, although exceptions exist. Some skippers, for example, have long proboscises, and some swallowtails have short ones. Most butterflies that seldom feed on nectar, such as certain satyrs and nymphalids, have very small proboscises.

Other floral characteristics also determine which butterflies visit which plants. Botanist Douglas Schemske observed butterflies that visited two species of lantana on the Osa Peninsula in Costa Rica. Large butterflies used *Lantana camara,* the flower head of which forms a wide, rounded platform. Small butterflies visited *Lantana trifolia,* the flowers of which sit on top of an elongate inflorescence, resulting in a narrow landing platform. While *L. camara* inflorescences have twice as many nectar flowers as those of *L. trifolia,* the former's corolla length is twice that of the latter. This excludes small butterflies, most of which have small proboscises, from drinking nectar at *L. camara.* Schemske hypothesizes that since the main pollinators of lantana are butterflies, these two plants evolved their present forms to separate their pollinators and ensure their own sympatric survival.

The importance of floral morphology in relation to butterfly visitation applies to other flowers besides lantana. Swallowtails, for instance, have an easier time using the platform of a daylily or a geranium than they do a low-lying alyssum. However, a cluster of small flowers on a stem, such as lantana, may be acceptable. The larger the flower, the more nectar it generally has. But small flowers situated in clusters allow butterflies to extend their proboscises to many flowers without moving off the cluster. Large flowers tend to be situated higher than small flowers, so large butterflies are often seen higher on plants than small butterflies. The height of a flower also gives them room for their large wings, which swallowtails flutter while they feed. Small butterflies often cannot cope with a large flower, either because of their short proboscis or because

Polydamas Swallowtail

they can't or won't climb down into the flower. Most butterflies seldom climb into flowers, because their wings are very sensitive to confinement and manipulation, but sometimes when they're particularly ravenous they'll bury their head in the flower in order to reach the nectar. Some species, including certain blues, take advantage of larger corollas by folding back their wings and burrowing down to reach the nectaries.

When a butterfly gets close to a flower, the flower's scent draws it in even more. Indeed, some of the most fragrant flowers, such as heliotrope, mignonette, lilac, lavender, sweet alyssum, and viburnum, often abound with butterflies. There is no telling whether butterflies smell things as we do. The fact that unsavory substances such as scat attracts them so would indicate otherwise. However, there is no question that scent plays a major role for butterflies in food selection.

Many flowers have nectar guides in the non-ultraviolet portion of the spectrum. These lines and patterns usually point to the center of the flower, where the nectaries occur, or they surround it. For instance, the yellow area in the center of many daisies, the dark-pink patch in the middle of some phloxes, and the lines leading to the center of certain cosmos, impatiens, and lilies, all serve this purpose. When butterflies drink nectar from flowers, they pollinate them by transferring pollen grain from stamen to stigma. This reward causes flowers to evolve nectar and nectar guides.

Because many variables operate in the area of butterfly nectar preferences, you'll have the best chance of pleasing your butterfly customers if you stock your "soda fountain" with nectar sources that feature a variety of shapes, sizes, colors, and fragrances. And since nectar sources come from all categories of plants you'll be using—including cultivated plants, native plants, shrubs, and trees, as well as larval foodplants—they will work well in many areas of your garden. By planting nectar sources in ornamental flower beds, meadows, foodplant areas, and wherever else you choose, you will have something for thirsty butterflies in each part of your garden.

If you ask butterfly gardeners which nectar sources they consider the most popular, they will probably select buddleia (or butterfly bush), orange milkweed (or butterfly weed), and lantana. But butterflies flock to many other flowers, including daisies, asters and other composites, lobelia, sweet alyssum, verbena, phlox, scabiosa, and coreopsis. Anyone who has spent time in meadows and fields knows that wildflowers such as goldenrod, Joe-Pye weed, boneset, wild bergamot, and dandelion have a magnetic effect on nectar-seeking butterflies. In addition to planting these flowers in your butterfly garden, you might want to include wild varieties of cultivated plants such as phlox, verbena, and aster. The flowers of shrubs and trees such as hawthorn, sumac, lilac, buckeye, and New Jersey tea also attract butterflies. And you'll no doubt observe butterflies drinking nectar from such larval foodplants as clover, buckwheat, and thistle.

Monarch

Since butterflies fly from spring until fall, and longer in warmer areas, you'll want to provide nectar sources for as long as the butterflies are around. Therefore, you should choose some spring-blooming flowers, such as arabis, primrose, and lilac; some summer-blooming flowers, such as butterfly weed and yarrow; and some late summer or early fall nectar sources, such as butterfly bush, goldenrod, and showy stonecrop. Some nectar flowers, such as candytuft, bloom from spring through summer; some, such as phlox, from summer into fall; and some, such as dandelion, all the way from spring to fall. In order to prolong the blooming season of your plants, you can prune them periodically. The plant will form a new flower head to compensate. This technique can extend the blooming season of butterfly bush from four weeks to twelve.

You should use both annual and perennial nectar sources in your butterfly garden. Annuals such as sweet alyssum, viper's bugloss, and mignonette can be moved from year to year, thus changing the look of your garden, while perennials such as sweet rocket, fleabane, and thrift will give your garden a feeling of stability. Gardens, of course, constantly change. Some perennials may die off in certain places, while annuals and perennials might start up from seeds scattered by an established plant. Since some perennials may not flower the first year, it pays to be patient with them. Nectar sources that come in both annual and perennial forms include candytuft, coreopsis, impatiens, lobelia, lupine, phlox, dianthus, sage, scabiosa, statice, sunflower, and toadflax.

One butterfly garden I visited in Los Angeles had a good combination of annual and perennial nectar sources. Along with perennials such as oleander, impatiens, and lantana, the garden featured a bed of annuals such as marigolds, cosmos, ageratum, dianthus, and dwarf zinnias, as well as a row of potted pansies. During my visit to this garden, I saw Fiery Skippers drinking nectar from the marigolds and a Funereal Duskywing taking nectar from cosmos flowers. A Cabbage White had laid some eggs on the nasturtium, the flowers of which also supplied the butterflies with nectar. Flower colors in the garden included pink, red, blue, yellow, orange, purple, lavender, and white.

Planning out your butterfly garden's color patterns will give you a chance to stretch your creativity and satisfy your aesthetic tastes. If you want vast stretches of white, purple, and rosy-red, plant ground covers such as alyssum, candytuft, and sedum. Gold and crimson multicolored gaillardias function as an attractive border, as do the more simple yellow or orange marigolds. I am constantly amazed at how soothing it feels to gaze at the fluffy, blue flower heads of ageratum, which make a pretty border, edging, or ground cover. Some gardeners fill their front yards with exquisite pink and yellow Michaelmas daisies, white and yellow Shasta daisies, or both. I am particularly fond of the Felicia daisy, with its yellow center and deep-lavender ray flowers. You might want to plant two species of lantana—yellow and orange *Lantana camara,* and light-purple *Lantana montevidensis*—right next to each other. An extremely functional plant, lantana will serve as a shrub or a ground cover. You might also want to choose the colors of your nectar sources in relation to the color of your house, the fence around your garden, and the colors of the butterflies you wish to attract.

Flower beds offer wonderful opportunities to combine colors. If you plant a combination of lavender, pink, and white phlox, you will have a variety of color, and constancy of form. By adding the orange flowers of butterfly weed, you will create splashes of brightness. Red geraniums and the tiny, yellow flowers of goldenrod will fill out the colors in your bed. And if you top it all off with the round, pink or purple flower heads of thistle, you will have a flower bed rich with various colors and forms.

Another option is to fill a flower bed with lots of the same kind of plant, of differing colors. Pink, white, blue, and red phlox work well in this manner, as does white, pink, or red sweet William. You might also want to design your garden around one particular color, such as lavender or yellow, or around a group of colors, such as pastels like light-blue and pink. Vita Sackville-West's famous White Garden at Sissinghurst Castle Gardens in Kent, England, still features butterfly nectar sources such as candytuft, lilies, dianthus, pansies, and irises. If you want an all-yellow butterfly garden, you might want to use such flowers as anthemis, marigold, sunflower, goldenrod, black-eyed Susan, beggar-ticks, buttercup, dandelion, common groundsel, ragwort, and toadflax. For a pink or red garden, use dianthus, phlox, scabiosa, bleeding heart, red campion, and primrose. A blue or purple garden could be effected with ageratum, globe thistle, lobelia, lavender, lupine, verbena, salvia, violets, wild berga-mot, and Joe-Pye weed.

You will stand a much better chance of attracting the butterflies you want if you plant a considerable clump of nectar sources, either the same flower or a combination, in each location. A solitary plant will not be nearly as enticing as a whole batch. Shrubs like butterfly bush are especially effective because they provide a color attractant over a wide area. This appears as a large blotch of color to the butterfly, which might lose sight of a solitary flower in the distance. Furthermore, the concentration of flower heads means more nectar for the butterflies and the more prone they'll be to stay.

Place nectar sources in the sun. A large proportion of your nectar supply should receive sunshine from mid-morning until mid-afternoon—the prime butterfly flying time. Some flowers might take in only the morning, midday, or afternoon sun. Butterflies gather nectar in the morning, afternoon, or all day, depending on the species. In order to accommodate them, your nectar sources should be in the sun at different times of the day.

Since plants produce nectar as a product of photosynthesis, the healthier they are, the more (and better) nectar they'll produce. Therefore, in addition to giving them plenty of sunlight, make sure they are watered well and have suitable soil in which to grow. Some plants produce nectar in the morning, some in the afternoon, and some all day. If early-rising bees or flies visit a morning-producing flower, a butterfly visiting that same flower after them might come up empty and will hurry off to the next prospect.

You should place trees and shrubs in corners and along the sides of the garden, so they don't shade out your flowers. Shrubs placed close to the house will soften the lines of the building, and perhaps make it look more natural to butterflies. If you plant some flowers next to the shrubs, you will soften and brighten the vista even more. A row of flowers or a pair of trees or shrubs will highlight the entrance to a section of your garden. For instance, if you want to highlight a butterfly bush and a small fountain in the middle of an open area, plant a row of nectar flowers leading up to the entrance, and a shrub or tree on either side. These could be nectar sources such as honeysuckle, buttonbush, wild plum, or wild cherry. They'll frame the area in the center and draw attention to your butterfly bush.

By placing potted nectar flowers into niches along a garden wall, fence, or patio railing, you will bring the flowers up to a higher level so they're easier for the butterflies to see and reach. If you place them next to a foodplant tree such as birch, the Eastern Tiger Swallowtails whose caterpillars feed on the leaves of these trees and whose females lay eggs on them will not have to flutter down to the ground for their nectar. You might even save some butterflies from predation this way, by keeping them from flying across the open expanse of your garden. Urban dwellers can place potted nectar sources on patios and in window boxes. A window box with brightly colored primroses, zinnias, verbena, and alyssum will attract Painted Ladies and other butterflies across paved streets to the oasis of your apartment windowsill.

At a butterfly garden in El Monte, California, a purple *Lantana montevidensis* covered the top and most of the sides of a corner of about a six-foot-high wire fence, as well as most of the fence along one side of the garden. While I was there, lots of skippers, Cabbage Whites, and Gulf Fritillaries drank nectar at the lantana, no doubt led to it in part because it was situated higher than the other flowers in the garden.

It is very important to observe your nectar sources continually. See which flowers butterflies visit, and which they avoid. Try to determine the primary ingredient of attraction. If a butterfly goes more often to one plant of the same color than another, it may be the shape of the flower, the fragrance, or the amount of nectar in the flower. Perhaps it prefers one color over another of the same flower species. Then you'll know to plant more of the popular color.

In a remarkable series of articles in *The Entomologist's Monthly Magazine*, A. H. Hamm recorded his extensive tabulations of butterfly visitors to a 200-yard border of closely interspersed reddish-purple, purple (pale to very dark) and white Michaelmas daisies on the grounds of the Cowley Road Hospital in Oxford, England. For five years starting in 1943, Hamm observed Red Admirals, Commas, Small Whites, Clouded Yellows, Small Tortoiseshells, and other species at these flowers during part of September and October. He reports that the reddish-purple flowers were preferred until the beginning or middle of October, when they became overblown. Then the various shades of purple flowers were chosen. The white forms were consistently neglected.

Observations such as these provide butterfly gardeners, entomologists, and other interested people with valuable, often rare information. Butterfly gardeners should therefore share their findings with each other. In addition to telling your neighbors about a nectar source you've found useful, you might want to contribute an article about it to an entomological journal. By communicating with other butterfly gardeners and by reading the latest news on the subject, you will extend your knowledge far beyond the walls of your garden.

As stated earlier, some butterflies, such as the White Admiral, Red-spotted Purple, Question Mark, Mourning Cloak, Red Admiral, Eastern Comma, and Viceroy, often eschew nectar sources in favor of substances such as rotting fruit, tree sap, dung, carrion, urine, and other wastes, from which they suck up essential nutrients. If you let the fruit from your fruit trees decay on the ground, this might attract some butterflies.

If you don't have any fruit trees (or even if you do), try placing some sliced oranges, cantaloupe, and bananas on a plate or tray in the garden. A wide variety of butterflies will love sucking up the juices from these fruits, as well as from strawberries, peaches, nectarines, watermelon, plums, pears, grapefruit, apples, or grapes.

In addition to providing butterflies with flowers, you might want to treat them to some sugar water by placing a sponge on a plate or tray and then saturating the sponge with the sugar water. You could place a number of these plates around your garden, and if you use sponges and plates of various colors, you might attract the butterflies even more. The sugar water should consist of a ten-to-one solution of water and white granulated sugar. I use filtered hot water from my kitchen faucet, into which I stir the sugar in a measuring cup. Then I pour that solution into a plastic pint container and store the container in the refrigerator until the following day. You may want to boil the solution until the sugar is dissolved. If you add some extra water to the solution before you boil it, you can be sure that the mixture is not stronger than ten-to-one after boiling. Sugar water can be stored in the refrigerator for a week or so. You may also

Gulf Fritillary (left) and Julia Heliconian (right)

want to try one of the commercially available butterfly feeders, which look similar to hummingbird feeders and have areas where fruit such as bananas and watermelon can be placed as well.

But in the end, butterfly gardening is really all about the flowers and the butterflies.

Ethel Anderson, a butterfly gardener in Australia, wrote in *The Atlantic Monthly* in August, 1940, that the butterflies far outnumbered the flowers in her garden. "I can see five Satyridae to each single dandelion. And on these lawns dandelions flourish like buttercups in Berkshire." Referring to the "fluttering thousands," she reported that "Penciled Blues and Fiery Jewels dance above the China asters, and over the cactus dahlias Clover Blues and Painted Ladies weave flight patterns prodigal in beauty.... On a Michaelmas daisy's lacy white and gold and green, three to a flower, wings up like sails, banked thick as Silver-washed Fritillaries in an English lane, succeeding fleets of Checkered Swallowtails ride at anchor, but are never still."

Then she adds, "If I were very rich, I would not have in my garden so very many trees (though I would have a good many), or flowers (though

I would have some, planted like vegetables in a kitchen garden)—no; I would keep a scientist to procure me flights of butterflies.

"Every morning I should like my butler to say, 'The scientist, ma'am, is on the back doorstep, awaiting today's orders.' Then I would answer, 'Tell him, please, to release on the perennial phlox fifty Tailed Cupids. Over the Prunus he could set free some Jezebels and Wood Whites, and take a covey of Lacewings and Leopards across to those hawthorns.'"

Most of us, like Anderson, do not have a scientist handy to procure for ourselves flights of butterflies—and fortunately, we do not need one. As we have seen, half the trick of bringing butterflies to your garden comes in having a well-stocked bar. After drinks comes the main course—the caterpillars' foodplants. And that is what we will discuss next.

Gulf Fritillary

CHAPTER 6

Larval Foodplants

"**I'm not a green thumb**, but I'm rather excited about growing a butterfly garden this spring in our backyard," *Los Angeles Times* columnist Jack Smith begins his column "A Passion for Butterflies." He had just learned that passion flower serves as the foodplant for the Gulf Fritillary. "I thought back to springs past," Smith writes, "when I had fought savagely but in vain against the passion vine that was violating our lovely pepper tree, seducing it with purple flowers and squeezing it lifeless in irresistible arms....And all the time...the passion vine was surrendering its own flesh to my caterpillars, and in time it would be transformed into the lovely orange, black and silver fritillary that gave such color and motion to our acre....I went down to look at the pepper tree, on our second level just at the edge of the canyon, to see if the vine was back. I hoped so. I hated to think of a summer without butterflies."

As we have discussed, butterflies employ a wide range of foodplants (both native and cultivated), including flowers, herbs, grasses, vegetables, shrubs, and trees. Some butterflies feed on foodplants from many different families, others from various members of the same family, and some from only one genus or even species of plant. Some small blues have co-evolved so closely with certain species of buckwheat that they use them exclusively for foodplant and nectar source alike. Most of the butterflies in our "Fifty North American Garden Butterflies" section feed on a range of foodplants, either within the same family or in different families. Those that feed on only one foodplant tend to use a plant that has a wide range.

Many butterflies (often those that are closely related) feed on the same or closely related foodplants. These include the Monarch and

Queen (milkweeds); many whites (members of the mustard family); the Great Spangled Fritillary and other fritillaries (violets); the Painted Lady and Mylitta Crescent (thistles); the Pearl Crescent and other crescents and checkerspots (asters); the Orange Sulphur, Southern Dogface, and other sulphurs (clovers); the Red Admiral, Eastern Comma, Question Mark, and Satyr Comma (nettles); the Black Swallowtail and Anise Swallowtail (members of the carrot family); and the Viceroy, White Admiral, and Red-spotted Purple (willows).

Butterflies that use a wide variety of foodplants, such as the Gray Hairstreak, Common Buckeye, Painted Lady, Eastern Comma, and Mourning Cloak, may select a certain host in a given area. Indeed, some foodplants grow better in certain regions than in others, and this will likely determine which foodplant a butterfly uses in that region. Also, some butterflies use a certain foodplant for their first brood in the spring and another for their second brood. For instance, the Spring Azure lays its eggs between the flower buds of its foodplant, and the larvae feed on the buds and flowers of that plant. Since the flowering periods of its foodplants are staggered, each generation of the Spring Azure chooses a different combination of foodplants. In northern Virginia, first-generation Spring Azure females choose common dogwood and wild cherry, while second-generation females choose New Jersey tea, osier dogwood, and viburnum. The succulence of a foodplant also determines whether (and when) a butterfly can utilize it. In the Sierra Nevada, for instance, the Edith's Checkerspot chooses certain species of the snapdragon family during the spring, and others in the summer. By summertime, the spring plants have dried out.

For three years, Larry Orsak studied the foodplant preferences of the Bright Blue Copper (*Lycaena heteronea clara*) in the Mount Pinos region, north of Los Angeles. Orsak discovered that of the 65 buckwheat species in Southern California, only three were selected by this butterfly—California buckwheat (*Eriogonum fasciculatum*); Heermann's buckwheat (*E. heermannii*); and sulphur-flower buckwheat (*E. umbellatum*). He states that since the butterfly seems always to lay its eggs deep within the foodplant in shaded leaf sites, it rejects sparsely leaved, low-growing buckwheats that provide neither shade nor shelter. Furthermore, when

Heermann's buckwheat and sulphur-flower buckwheat each grow alone alongside common buckwheat, the butterfly overwhelmingly favors the former two. This, Orsak says, is because the females strongly prefer large leaves on which to lay their eggs—and Heermann's buckwheat has larger leaves than sulphur-flower buckwheat, which has larger leaves than California buckwheat.

The habitat in which a foodplant grows also affects its condition, and hence its suitability for ovipositing females. According to Orsak, California buckwheat that grows on canyon floors receives more water, puts out more growth, and has much larger leaves than California buckwheat that grows on adjacent arid south slopes. "Correspondingly," he states, "the Bright Blue Copper is found on the canyon floors but never on the south slopes."

In your butterfly garden, you should provide a steady supply of fresh foodplants for each butterfly species. If a butterfly is double-brooded, you need suitable food for the second generation as well as the first. Imagine inviting birds to your garden, and then running out of food in the feeder. The principle also applies to butterflies. With species like the Cabbage White, providing the proper foodplant requires little planning. But the Baltimore Checkerspot feeds on turtlehead in northern regions, and uses beardtongue in the South. Furthermore, while Baltimore Checkerspot larvae feed on these plants prior to overwintering, they may wander off and use a wide range of unrelated plants (including white ash and Japanese honeysuckle) when they resume feeding in the spring.

In order to determine which foodplant or foodplants work best for each butterfly you want to attract, you should make some observations in your local area regarding the favorites of each butterfly. Consult with other butterfly gardeners and find out which foodplants they consider popular. National and regional field guides (as well as this book) contain information on foodplant preferences; and local lists compiled by natural history museums and amateur entomologists often have valuable first-hand information.

Sometimes the "official" preference of a particular butterfly will not be the one it favors in your area. For instance, the Painted Lady is commonly said to prefer thistles, but it might use mallow where you live. The Viceroy prefers willows, but it might favor poplar or aspen in your area. The Eastern Comma consumes hops and nettles, but it might choose elm in your vicinity. By keeping your eyes open for local preferences, you will be best prepared to provide for the butterflies.

Cultivated plants that serve as foodplants (and some of the butterflies that use them) include nasturtium (Cabbage White), hibiscus (Gray Hairstreak), violets (fritillaries), spicebush (Spicebush Swallowtail), hawthorn (White Admiral, Red-spotted Purple), senna (Cloudless Sulphur, Orange-barred Sulphur, Sleepy Orange), hollyhock (Painted Lady), and passion flower (Gulf Fritillary). Trees such as elm (Mourning Cloak, Question Mark), willow (Viceroy, Eastern Comma), sycamore (Western Tiger Swallowtail), pawpaw (Zebra Swallowtail), and various citrus species (Giant Swallowtail) provide large leafy areas for hungry caterpillars. In addition to native grasses, common lawn varieties such as Bermuda grass and St. Augustine grass sustain a number of satyrs and skippers.

Milkweed, thistle, and nettle are good examples of wildflowers that are used as foodplants. Rather than spraying or rooting them out, butterfly gardeners who wish to see Monarchs, Painted Ladies, and Red Admirals should tolerate, even nurture these plants. L. Hugh Newman states, "Usually nothing more than a little neglect is needed in order to establish a nettlebed." Newman suggests placing nettlebeds "somewhere by the rubbish heap near the garden shed," and he states that if butterfly gardeners leave the window or door of the shed open, some of the hibernating butterflies that use the nettles (such as the Peacock and Small Tortoiseshell) may spend the winter inside the shed. "Then in the spring, when they wake up again and come out to feed, a nettlebed in the sun just round the corner may very well seem inviting enough for a female to settle there to lay her large batch of green eggs." Newman was at "constant 'war'" with the head gardener at Sir Winston Churchill's Chartwell estate, who wanted to clear the grounds of all nettlebeds. Eventually they reached an "amicable" agreement. "Certain nettlebeds became sacrosanct to the butterflies, and the rest were kept within bounds."

Orange-barred Sulphur

Other wildflowers that serve as foodplants (and some butterflies that use them) include lupine (Boisduval's Blue, Silvery Blue); plantain (Common Buckeye); cresses (Sara and Falcate Orangetips); pearly everlasting (American Lady); vetches (Eastern and Western Tailed-Blues); and sorrel and dock (American and Purplish Coppers). Many foodplants that grow wild, such as asters, lupines, violets, thistles, milkweeds, clovers, and carrots, have cultivated varieties. Not all of these cultivated plants may be suitable. For example, a Silvery Blue female may not be willing to oviposit on a Russell lupine.

You might want to incorporate some foodplants into a vegetable or herb garden. If you plant enough of each foodplant, you should have an ample supply for the butterflies and for yourself. Vegetables and herbs especially good for attracting butterflies include: cabbage, broccoli, and collards for the whites; carrot, parsley, dill, and celery for the Black Swallowtail; alfalfa for the Orange Sulphur; beans for the Gray Hairstreak; and mallow for the Painted Lady and West Coast Lady. Orange and other citrus trees will attract the Giant Swallowtail; apple trees will bring in the Eastern Tiger Swallowtail; and hops will draw in the Question Mark, Eastern Comma, and Red Admiral. If you want to save particular plants from being eaten, put some netting around them so the female can't lay eggs on them, or pick off the caterpillars and put them on the plants you want them to eat. Most butterfly gardeners find it a simple matter to grow enough to share.

When working with foodplants, you should use the areas adjacent to your garden as an extension of it. For instance, if the house next door has a tall elm tree, there's no need for you to grow one, especially considering how long it takes for any tree to become full-grown. But by planting a new tree, you'll be able to see the caterpillars and butterflies better since they'll be closer to the ground when the tree is young. Indeed, you could plant sassafras (for the Spicebush Swallowtail) and pawpaw (for the Zebra Swallowtail), since these butterflies feed on very young trees. However, the Eastern Tiger Swallowtail oviposits so high up in its foodplant trees that its egg-laying females, caterpillars, and eggs are often difficult to see.

If you live near a forest, prairie, or other wild area, you can use these habitats to complement your garden. Mustard or buckwheat seeds collected from a nearby meadow should thrive in your yard. Adjacent wild areas also serve as a source of butterfly immigrants and offer opportunities for gathering eggs, larvae, and pupae. Just be sure not to disturb rare wild plants.

If you interact with your local surroundings while providing your own foodplants and nectar sources, you'll have the best of both worlds. My house in Los Angeles overlooks a canyon in which the Western Tiger Swallowtail feeds on California sycamore; the Anise Swallowtail on fennel; the California Sister on coast live oak; the "California" Common Ringlet on grasses; the Lorquin's Admiral on willow; and the Cabbage

White on mustard. My garden contains daisies, marigolds, star clusters, lily of the Nile, and other nectar sources which attract butterflies such as the Marine Blue, Gulf Fritillary, Gray Hairstreak, Fiery Skipper, Umber Skipper, West Coast Lady, and Funereal Duskywing.

When planting foodplants, especially wildflowers, you should try to approximate the natural habitat of those plants, in terms of the amount of sun and water they get, and what type of soil they like. According to Bernard Jackson, moist environments occur naturally in the Memorial University of Newfoundland Botanical Garden for willows, alders, violets, and cranberry—foodplants for the Mourning Cloak, Green Comma, fritillaries, and Bog Copper respectively. "Most of these plants can be grown in the home garden by increasing the soil's capability to retain moisture," Jackson states. He suggests adding lots of moisture-retentive material such as peat moss or leaf mold but stresses that "good drainage is still important. If a small cranberry bog is required, such a site can be made by forming a shallow saucer of plastic sheeting a foot below ground level and filling it with shredded peat. A hole must be cut

Western Tiger Swallowtail

Cabbage White

Marine Blue

Gray Hairstreak

in the plastic at the lowest point of the 'bog,' otherwise too much water will be retained."

Jackson recalls that at one time, many of the alders and willows in the garden became spindly after being smothered by nearby trees. After trimming back the area to give the alders and willows more sun, and cutting them to ground level to encourage new, fuller growth, the plants responded quickly, and Jackson began to see more Green Commas and Mourning Cloaks in the garden. "Such habitat improvement, and the maintenance of this work, is continuous," he states.

Umber Skipper

Cudweed, a foodplant of the American Lady, grows in habitats such as barren roadsides, to a height of about two inches. But in a garden with rich soil, it will double this height. Thus, you could plant cudweed in a sunny corner as a border. American Lady caterpillars eat cudweed buds and then move to new plants. In boom years, they often over-crowd small, roadside plants, and many caterpillars starve. Large, healthy cudweed plants in butterfly gardens could help American Lady larvae survive during these years.

You shouldn't cut your foodplants too much. If you let them grow out, they will be large enough to resist being destroyed by caterpillars, and they'll also look more natural. If all the foodplants in your garden grow out well, the whole place will look that much more natural to the butterflies. And the more natural your garden looks to butterflies, the better chance you'll have of attracting them. You might want to trim your foodplants occasionally, however, in order to provide new, tender growth for new broods of caterpillars.

Bunches of foodplants should be planted in the same area. This will attract more butterflies than a solitary plant. Just as a number of nectar flowers will support more butterflies than a single flower, a patch of foodplants will support more caterpillars than a single plant. Since caterpillars have fewer food choices than adults, and female butterflies have a limited selection of plants on which to lay eggs, you should provide an ample supply of each type of foodplant for each species. Of course, butterflies will come to just one plant, but why not be prepared for more?

In their book *The Butterflies of Southern California*, Thomas Emmel and John Emmel report that in some years, considerable numbers of Painted Ladies migrate north from Mexico and join large populations of Painted Ladies that have appeared in the Southern California deserts after heavy winter rains. These millions of butterflies then fly north and east throughout North America. In the spring of 1983, so many Painted Ladies migrated through San Diego from Mexico that alarmed San Die-gans phoned the local newspaper asking if the insects that were alighting on their flowers and vegetables were harmful. No doubt some butterfly gardeners in San Diego were caught unprepared that year.

If you run low on a foodplant, you should be able to get more at that time, especially during butterfly season. If not, you'll know to plant enough next season. Since butterflies appear in an unpredictable fashion, a given foodplant may not attract any butterflies one year, but the next they might flock to it. One simple rule regarding how much of each foodplant you should have is this: Better too much than too little.

Most butterfly gardeners place foodplants alongside nectar sources in beds on the sides of their garden. But you might want to let some foodplants grow in your lawn. Instead of killing the clover that naturally establishes itself there, you could let it grow and attract beautiful sulphurs and tailed-blues. Clover also serves as a superb nectar source for Tawny Skippers, Gray Hairstreaks, and other butterflies. Cudweed often colonizes lawns. If you get rid of the cudweed, you might have a tidier lawn, but you won't enjoy seeing the American Lady in your yard. As a monoculture, a lawn provides a limited vista; but as a butterfly pasture, a lawn area can be richly rewarding, yet still aesthetically pleasing.

As discussed in Chapter Four, you might want to leave a portion of your lawn unmowed, or even the whole lawn, so as to give your garden a hayfield look. Foodplants as well as nectar sources will flourish among the tall grasses. If you are a suburban gardener, be prepared to defend the practice as ecologically and aesthetically valuable. Some of the more aggressive foodplants, when potted, will not spread as rapidly and take over other areas. And if you cut off the flower heads of these plants before they go to seed, you will prevent them from establishing new plants in your garden or in your neighbors' yards.

One butterfly gardener I visited had a meadow for a front yard. It contained tall grasses; wildflowers such as fennel, milkweed, Queen Anne's lace, and dandelion; and cultivated flowers including verbena, daisies, gaillardia, geranium, phlox, and violets. The other houses on his street had traditional lawns, but this individual was unperturbed. "I was gonna have a meadow here," he said, "and by George, now I have a meadow." Didn't his neighbors complain, I asked? "Some people have," he said, "but not my immediate neighbors. They're used to it." As we stood there, Cabbage Whites, West Coast Ladies, Gulf Fritillaries, Marine Blues, and Fiery Skippers flew around us. This person had a vegetable garden in his backyard that contained such foodplants as alfalfa, mallow, cabbage, and dill. A large passion flower vine flanked one side of the vegetable garden.

In the Midwest, many gardeners use native prairie grasses instead of Kentucky bluegrass. These grasses require no irrigation and nurture prairie insects, birds, and small mammals, as well as butterflies. At the Schlitz Audubon Nature Center in Milwaukee, the mix of forested and grassland habitat includes many foodplants for the butterflies as well as nectar sources such as New Jersey tea, butterfly weed, blazing star, and ironweed.

Certain showy foodplants, such as milkweed, thistle, aster, lupine, violets, and everlastings, will fit right in with the ornamental flowers in your beds. You might want to place weedy foodplants, such as nettles, behind your nectar sources, so they're not readily visible to the casual observer. The butterflies, though, will no doubt find them. Many larval foodplants don't have as showy flowers as nectar sources, but have attractive qualities of their own. The silvery-gray leaves of pearly everlasting make a beautiful counterpoint to the darker green foliage of other plants, be they nectar sources or foodplants. The thin, lacy leaves of herbs such as fennel will give your garden a feeling of levity. Fennel and other members of the carrot family have attractive and captivating, umbrella-shaped flower heads. And everyone knows how soothing the light, wavy appearance of flowering grasses can be.

Foodplant trees and shrubs shouldn't shade out your nectar sources. Like nectar sources, most foodplants should be placed in the sun. But they shouldn't be too detectable to predators such as birds, which might easily see caterpillars on a solitary plant standing in the middle of an open lawn. Therefore, you might want to place your foodplants along the side of the garden. In the butterfly garden at the Drum Manor Forest Park, the south-facing stone wall absorbs and emits heat from the sun, thereby creating a sun trap that features higher temperatures than would ordinarily exist under direct radiation. Because of this, foodplants in the garden have a longer growing season. This technique would be especially useful for foodplants on the perimeters of butterfly gardens, since they shouldn't be too exposed, but should still receive enough heat and sun.

Since oviposition behavior varies from species to species, you should place each butterfly's foodplants in the optimal environment to induce egg laying. Some butterflies will fly into dappled sunlight and even shade in order to lay their eggs—perhaps because they sense that this will give the eggs some protection from predators and the baking sun. Others will only oviposit in direct sun. If you plant some foodplants in different areas, you should be able to determine which environment each species prefers.

As stated earlier, butterfly gardens should have plenty of shelter for butterflies. You might want to concentrate on foodplant trees and shrubs for this purpose. To me, an ideal butterfly garden would have Mourning Cloaks flying down from elm trees; Western Tiger Swallowtails floating around California sycamores; Gray Hairstreaks perching on hibiscus; Lorquin's Admirals appearing from willow stands; and Gulf Fritillaries cavorting, as they seem to do, around passion-flower-covered fences.

If you care for your foodplants properly, and for the caterpillars that feed on them, the larvae will have a much better chance of surviving. Fine-mesh netting around the stems and branches of foodplants, or over entire plants, will protect the eggs, caterpillars, and pupae on them from birds and spiders. Make sure the netting is fine enough so that small spiders and wasps can't get in. To put netting on a branch (or stem), make a sleeve that's open at both ends. Slip it onto the branch and tie it tightly on each end. You should empty the sleeve regularly of the caterpillar droppings (frass) that accumulate. To do this, unwind the string on the lower side of the branch and tap the frass out. Be careful not to unseat the caterpillars. If the caterpillars eat up the leaves on one branch, move them to another and put the sleeve around it. If you want caterpillars to pupate and hatch in these enclosures, make sure they have enough room. (You can also purchase fine mesh rearing sleeves that you can place over the stems of your foodplants.)

Foodplants placed under trellises and canopies will be less visible to birds and less damaged by rain. You might want to put a fine-mesh cage around a bunch of foodplants, or put them into a large, fine-mesh enclosure, either one that you build or one that you purchase. By potting foodplants, you will be able to place them in an outdoor cage or on a porch to minimize the danger to larvae; or move the plants into a more environmentally suitable location, such as into or out of the sun depending on whether they need more or less direct light. When I visited entomologist Rudi Mattoni, he showed me foodplants in various-sized pots on an east-facing, second-floor balcony at his home in Beverly Hills. Since he constantly experimented with foodplants, these pots provided a convenient way to add and subtract foodplants from his roster without having to plant them in his garden. And since the balcony was well exposed and received plenty of morning sun, the foodplants there attracted many butterflies from the surrounding area.

Spiders, mice, and other predators may find their way into porches, so you should put netting over your foodplants there if the screening isn't secure enough. You shouldn't let moisture accumulate on your foodplants, because this can help bacteria to breed, which will infect your caterpillars. Mold is also a big problem in damp spots and can be lethal to larvae. Remember to always water your foodplants from below, so you don't drown caterpillars, pupae, or eggs. In general, you will probably achieve the best results in caring for your foodplants and caterpillars if you simply apply common sense. If it seems as if a situation might pose a danger to the larvae—be it too much or too little moisture or heat, lack of ventilation, exposure to predators, or overcrowding—then take the appropriate action to remedy the situation. Even though caterpillars are hardy, they can be fragile at times, so it's better to be overly protective than to neglect them.

Like nectar sources, foodplants must be available during the time when each butterfly species is on the wing. With an early spring butterfly, the foodplant should already be established in your yard or the butterfly will wander off in search of a suitable place to lay eggs. Therefore, you should start early spring plants indoors before the last frost and then bring them out in pots or transplant them as soon as weather conditions allow.

Your choice of foodplants will give you a great deal of control over which butterflies visit your garden. If you want a wide variety of butterflies, plant a wide selection of foodplants. You might want to plant one foodplant that attracts a number of different butterflies, such as thistles for the Painted Lady and various crescents; wild cherry for the Eastern Tiger Swallowtail and Red-spotted Purple; poplar for the White Admiral and Viceroy; and nettles for the Red Admiral, Question Mark, and Eastern Comma. Or you might want to plant a number of different foodplants that only attract one butterfly (such as turtlehead for the Baltimore Checkerspot, and spicebush for the Spicebush Swallowtail); or a few related butterflies (such as milkweeds for the Monarch and Queen, and passion flower for the Gulf Fritillary and Zebra Heliconian). Most butterfly gardeners use a combination of foodplants. Which foodplants you use will depend on their availability, your own favorites, your location, and your luck at obtaining and growing them.

One butterfly gardener I visited in Los Angeles had a huge passion flower growing along a fence in his yard. The other sides of the yard were sheltered by the house, an unattached garage, a few trees, and a treehouse. In one corner of the garden, the passion flower rose fifteen to twenty feet, covering a Chinese elm. The plant dominated the garden, and aside from the lawn, it was the only foodplant there. It was also the only passion flower in the immediate vicinity, so it attracted plenty of Gulf Fritillaries.

Gulf Fritillary

While I was there, at least seven Gulf Fritillaries visited the passion flower. As a female sunned herself on one of the plant's blossoms, a male approached her. She ignored him, but when two more males arrived, she darted away and they all started chasing her around the yard. She flew evasively, but they followed closely. Eventually, she eluded them, or they gave up their pursuit. A short while later, I saw her laying eggs one at a time on the leaves of the passion flower. I was given a few sprigs of the plant, with eggs on the leaves, and I reared three caterpillars from them and released the butterflies when they emerged. This garden specialized in one foodplant, but it was as impressive a butterfly garden as any that I visited.

Cabbage White

CHAPTER 7

Butterfly Gardening Activities

Once present in the garden, butterflies afford a great array of pleasures. In addition to their beauty, they offer a wide range of attractions and activities. Only your imagination need limit the opportunities for exploring butterfly recreation.

Whether on a casual basis or on a more scientific level, observing various butterfly species at different stages of their life cycle allows you to appreciate their diversity of appearance and behavior, and perhaps make some valuable discoveries of your own. Whatever the extent of your involvement, you'll probably want to invest in some equipment, such as a butterfly net, a hand lens, a butterfly field guide, and a notebook in which to record your observations.

The butterfly net has several useful functions as a tool for butterfly gardeners. For instance, capturing butterflies will enable you to make accurate identifications, and to bring back females to lay eggs on your foodplants. In order to catch a butterfly, you should stalk it slowly and carefully, just as when you're watching it. If you wait for it to land, you'll have a better chance of netting it than if you flail away at the air, where the butterfly has a better chance to maneuver. If a butterfly lands on a flower or a perch above the ground, move your net swiftly across the plane of the butterfly, and be sure to flip the net over after making your pass, so the netting overlaps and traps the butterfly inside. With targets on the ground, clap the net over the butterfly and lift the top of the bag so the butterfly flies up into it. Whenever you try to catch a butterfly, make sure you swing the net swiftly enough so that the butterfly doesn't have a chance to react. You'll have the most success if you move slowly until just before making your strike. Approach flying butterflies from behind, as they can see and avoid objects in front of them adroitly.

One day, on a mountain road just north of Malibu, Rudi Mattoni made as expert a catch as I have witnessed. With his long-handled, small-bagged net in hand, he spied a tiny "Bernardino" Square-spotted Blue burst away from a buckwheat plant and into the middle of the road. Instantly, he sprinted after it and caught up. Using his wrists for strength, he slapped the net through the air a few times. I thought he might have missed, but there wasn't a trace of doubt on his face. Sure enough, a tiny blue fluttered in the net when he came back. What struck me about this was his single-mindedness and the directness of his strike. Once he anticipated the butterfly's flight pattern, he committed himself completely to his course of action.

When a butterfly is inside your net, be sure to handle the netting as carefully as possible. Butterflies are very fragile, and a movement that you wouldn't think harmful could break off a leg or do worse damage. You may be tempted to handle butterflies with your fingers. According to lepidopterist Robert Michael Pyle, spatulate stamp tongs work best for this purpose, since they lack sharp or serrated edges, which can damage wings. Pyle instructs butterfly handlers to clamp all four wings near their bases, making sure the legs are visible. This indicates that the wings are correctly situated over the butterfly's back. Pressing tightly will not harm the butterfly, and will prevent any of the wings from coming loose and tearing. Be sure your tongs don't grab part of the netting, or you might damage the butterfly's wings when you remove the butterfly from the net.

To release a butterfly, relax your grip on the tongs and the butterfly will fly away; or return it to its perch. If you want to bring a butterfly home safely, you should put it in one of the small glassine envelopes (similar to stamp envelopes) that butterfly collectors use. By keeping the butterflies slightly cool (you can put them in your cooler in the field), they will remain still and safe until you expose them to warmer temperature. Place the envelopes in a sturdy container until you get home.

Many years ago, at a Fourth of July butterfly count on the Palos Verdes Peninsula, I made my own butterfly net in about fifteen minutes.

I did this by fitting a pre-made butterfly net onto a circular piece of galvanized steel wire; bending back the two ends of the wire into lips a couple of inches long; and placing the lips into grooves on either side of a wooden dowel, which I pressed snugly into a ¾-inch-diameter, three-foot piece of PVC pipe. It gave me a feeling of satisfaction to know, every time I used my net, that I made it myself. You can purchase your own butterfly net as well. Just be sure that the handle isn't too flimsy, and that the net allows air to pass through it, so you can move the net swiftly.

A hand lens, or strong magnifying glass, will enable you to see butterfly anatomy, such as scales, up close. When viewed through a magnifying glass, a butterfly egg becomes a tall, shiny, striated, living thing, in which you can sense the makings of a butterfly; a butterfly's eyes appear as multi-faceted optical masterpieces; and its proboscis impresses you with its length and engineering. A pair of binoculars inverted serves the same purpose as a hand lens. Used in the usual way, binoculars enable you to watch wild butterflies at a distance without disturbing them, and to spot butterflies better in the field.

Some butterfly field guides cover all of North America, and some cover certain regions, states, and even cities. A guidebook will help you identify the species in your yard, especially those that look similar or have a subspecies that exists in your area alone. By reading through field guides at your leisure, you'll come across many facts and anecdotes about butterfly distribution, life-cycle characteristics, behavior, and coloration.

When observing and studying butterflies, it's helpful to keep a notebook, and it's important to be as accurate as possible. Write down your observations as soon after making them as you can, so as not to lose or confuse any information. For instance, while studying the color of a butterfly, you could look away for a few minutes and forget whether an area on it is orange with a tint of yellow, or yellow with a tint of orange. This could make a big difference when describing a butterfly.

By accurately observing salient field marks, such as the similar yet distinctive orange markings on the wing tips of the Lorquin's Admiral and California Sister, you will be able to match butterflies up with the photographs or illustrations of them in field guides. Some field guides use arrows to point out markings on butterflies that can be used to tell species and sexes apart. Roger Tory Peterson, an avid butterfly gardener as well as birdwatcher, developed this system of "field marks."

When I reared caterpillars, I tried to keep as detailed and accurate notes as possible regarding their daily, hourly, and even minute-by-minute behavior; time between moltings; and response to stimuli such as light, darkness, heat, wind (such as that caused by blowing on them), and touch (e.g., stroking them lightly with a fennel leaf). Sometimes this record-keeping becomes tedious, and occasionally I became so preoccupied with keeping a comprehensive record that there hardly seemed time for anything else. First-time butterfly observers will no doubt be tempted to record virtually everything they see. But after a while, you'll learn (for your own good) to write down only those observations germane to a particular course of study, or that stand out from other facts related to a particular species, or that distinguish a particular species from other butterflies.

Any observation you make and record has value. Some aspects to note include which species of a foodplant you saw a butterfly on in the field; which species of butterflies visit various nectar sources and foodplants; the date you collected the larvae of a particular species and how long it took to rear them to adulthood; how long each foodplant lasts when cut and put in water; how quickly each species of caterpillar eats its foodplants, and how much it consumes. Observations such as these will help you decide which butterflies you want to attract to your garden, and which foodplants and nectar sources you want to use. They will also be of value when you exchange information with other butterfly gardeners. Earliest and latest appearance, abundance, and sex ratios of butterfly visitors to your garden may also be recorded.

By constantly experimenting with and observing such factors as the fluctuations of butterfly populations, plant growth patterns, and environmental conditions, you will be able to react accordingly and continually increase the effectiveness of your butterfly garden. You may want to keep a record of how many individual butterflies and how many species visit or become established in your yard. You could compare your results from year to year to see how weather, your garden management and other factors affect butterfly populations. If you share your findings with other butterfly gardeners in your area, you could develop an overall "data bank" for your region. This information could be sent to your local natural history museum or entomology club. Although a great deal is known about butterflies, there is still an enormous amount to be learned, so any input, however small, is valuable.

As perhaps their first introduction to the biological and behavioral aspects of wildlife, a butterfly garden is especially valuable for young people. If a school started a butterfly garden on its premises, the garden would serve as an outdoor laboratory for students to study and tend. And because of their enthusiasm for chasing after and counting things, young people represent a valuable resource for conducting butterfly counts. If young people become involved in activities such as these, their parents may join them—or vice versa.

As part of the overall experience of observing and learning about butterflies, you might want to pay a visit to one of the many butterfly houses that are open to the public across the country. In Coconut Creek, Florida, Butterfly World has a campaign called "Bring Back the Butterflies," which encourages people to create butterfly gardens in order to encourage more butterflies back into their communities.

Other butterfly houses that are open to the public include the Cockrell Butterfly Center at the Houston Museum of Natural Science; the Puelicher Butterfly Wing at the Milwaukee Public Museum; the Sophia M. Sachs Butterfly House at the Missouri Botanical Garden in Chesterfield; and the Cecil B. Day Butterfly Center at Callaway Gardens in Pine Mountain, Georgia.

Butterfly houses such as these often include outdoor butterfly gardens on the grounds of the facilities, as the goal is to promote the conservation of these fabulous creatures. There are also many butterfly houses that are open to visitors in Europe, Asia, and Latin America, and the Melbourne Zoo in Australia has a butterfly house as well.

Taking photographs of butterflies is as gratifying to me as producing images of birds. First of all, there is the ethereal quality of it all. Butterflies make no noise as they fly around, so you feel as if you are in a magical place as you click away. You can photograph butterflies as they take nectar from a flower, in profile or from above. It is also interesting to get down and look up at the butterfly, especially if it is backlit. Maybe you want to try and capture an image of a butterfly in flight. That is quite a challenge, but it can be done. Just make sure your shutter speed is fast enough.

I also get a kick out of photographing the eggs, larvae, and pupae of butterflies. This involves using a macro lens, which allows you to focus from close up. But I use the macro lenses for photographing adult butterflies as well. I have had success using a 180mm macro lens, as well as a 100mm macro lens, but I have also used 50mm and 60mm macro lenses for butterfly photography, as well as my 100-400mm lens. I have even used my 18-135mm lens for butterfly photography and have had success with it, as with an image of two Giant Swallowtails taking nectar from a star clusters flower head (see page 14).

The key is to concentrate on your subject, focus properly, and make sure you have a fast enough shutter speed to catch these fast-moving animals before they fly off. You also have to take many photographs in order to get the ones that are in focus and have great compositions. In many ways, it requires more picture taking to get a great image of a butterfly than to get a great image of a bird. My best advice for butterfly photography is that when you see the moment through your viewfinder, do not hesitate. Click away, and worry about the details later. Butterfly moments are as fleeting as they appear to be. But preserving these moments in an image is extremely rewarding.

If you have artistic inclinations, you may want to try your hand at drawing or painting butterflies. See how many species you can depict, and see if your friends can tell which species you've drawn. Young people can outline the shapes of butterflies and their distinctive markings on a sheet of paper, and then color in the details; or you can use a butterfly coloring book.

You could also conduct a "caterpillar crawl," in which kids crawl across an area in the same manner as caterpillars, or you might want to make a Halloween costume depicting your favorite butterfly. All of these activities might inspire future lepidopterists.

Frank Lutz, former curator of the Department of Entomology at the American Museum of Natural History, authored *A Lot of Insects: Entomology in a Suburban Garden*, about his butterfly garden. Lutz described a "bargain that was not made" with the director of the museum, who refused to believe that at least 500 different insect species either visited or lived in Lutz's 75 × 200-foot suburban yard in Ramsey, New Jersey. Lutz told the director that if the museum increased his salary by ten dollars a year for every species above 500 that he found on his lot, he would agree to a salary reduction of ten dollars per year for every species under 500. The bet was never made official, but Lutz began counting . . . and counting. Eventually, he recorded 1402 species, including wasps, ants, bees, flies, beetles, moths, and 35 species of butterflies from six families, including the Great Spangled Fritillary, Pearl Crescent,

Gulf Fritillary

Giant Swallowtail

Great Southern White

Baltimore Checkerspot, Question Mark, Mourning Cloak, Red Admiral, American Lady, Common Buckeye, Red-spotted Purple, Viceroy, Gray Hairstreak, Spring Azure, Cabbage White, Clouded Sulphur, Black Swallowtail, Spicebush Swallowtail, and Eastern Tiger Swallowtail—all of which are in the "Fifty North American Garden Butterflies" section of this book. "My salary has not been increased," Lutz writes, "but I have had a lot of fun. So can you." Indeed, if he could see so much in his suburban lot, imagine what you could experience with a little effort and imagination in your own butterfly garden.

Spicebush Swallowtail

Orange-barred Sulphur

CHAPTER 8

How to Rear Butterflies

Rearing butterflies, an easy and rewarding activity, can enhance the enjoyment of one's butterfly garden immensely. First you'll need the butterflies themselves, which you should be able to gather in various stages of development from your garden and from places around your neighborhood or farther afield.

I find it very effective to watch a female oviposit, and then I can bring her eggs home to rear them. For one thing, it's easier to find a female in the wild than an egg. I also know (or at least I'm pretty sure) the eggs will be safe at home, and I feel intimately connected to each butterfly that results from one of these eggs.

When using this technique (or when collecting eggs on their own in the wild), be sure to bring home the stems with the leaves on which the butterfly has laid her eggs. If you immediately place these stems in water, the foodplant should remain fresh for a number of days, or, depending on the foodplant, as long as a week or two. Since eggs usually take about a week to hatch, this will provide the newly hatched caterpillars with fresh enough leaves on which to start feeding.

Many butterfly rearers capture a female and place her in a cage with some potted foodplant or cut foodplant in water. Most females will have mated by the time they're caught, so there's a good chance that any captured female will lay fertile eggs, usually within a day or so. Females usually require some sustenance to lay eggs, so be sure to provide plenty of fresh nectar blossoms (either from potted plants or cut stems in water), or a solution of sugar water presented on a sponge in a dish. Rearers like this method because it ensures them of a lot of eggs, with a minimum of collecting effort.

If you want to find caterpillars on a foodplant, look for leaves that have holes in them. Such feeding damage may give away the presence of caterpillars nearby. Inspect the undersides of leaves, where caterpillars often rest. As with eggs, caterpillars will be far safer in your home than in the wild. I witnessed an illustration of this one afternoon when collecting Gulf Fritillary caterpillars from a passion flower vine. Since I wanted to see the butterflies hatch soon, I only took late-instar larvae at first. Spying an early-instar caterpillar crawling on a leaf, I decided to wait until later to collect it. By then I would know if I had enough large ones. Also, since younger larvae are more fragile than older ones, I didn't want it to suffer any damage from being carried in my paper bag, which was partially filled with stems, leaves, and caterpillars. I returned to the tiny caterpillar about ten minutes later and had just set my gaze in the direction of the leaf when, out of the corner of my eye, a blurry object jumped forth and then disappeared. Inspecting the spot on the leaf where the caterpillar had been, I was shocked to see it gone. I couldn't tell if a spider or something else had gotten it, but I felt somehow to blame. If only I had picked it up when I first saw it, it would still have been alive.

When gathering eggs and larvae in the field, be on the lookout for evidence that distinguishes each species. Some butterflies, such as the Mourning Cloak, Compton Tortoiseshell, and Baltimore Checkerspot, lay their eggs in clusters and the caterpillars feed in groups. Young Baltimore Checkerspot larvae feed communally in silk nests until they're half-grown, and then they overwinter in rolled up leaves on the ground. The Viceroy and other admirals overwinter in hibernaculi, which they construct by curling the tip of a leaf of their foodplant and attaching the sides with silk that they spin. Many larvae, such as those of swallowtails, feed individually. You may visit a foodplant and find no evidence of butterflies there, but a week later, it might be covered with eggs and caterpillars, so keep checking.

Because they're so well camouflaged with their surroundings, chrysalises tend to be extremely difficult to find. That makes the reward greater, so you might want to try nonetheless. Look for chrysalises on the stems of foodplants and other nearby plants, and attached to walls, fences, logs, trees, and under the eaves of houses. Some butterflies wander farther than others before they pupate, and some prefer to pupate on their foodplant. Some like a particular substrate on which to pupate. This may be because they can blend in better with it. One butterfly gardener I visited in Santa Monica had a large patch of fennel growing alongside a weather-beaten wood fence. An Anise Swallowtail that had pupated on the fence blended in so well that from only a few feet away it was indistinguishable from the fence's gray, black, brown, and white patterns. Others of the same species form green pupae, since statistically the pupation substrate may be green or brown.

By getting to know the habits of the butterflies you wish to find, you will be best prepared for locating them. However, surprises can always occur. Most of the Gulf Fritillaries I reared in my apartment wandered around the rearing cage for a long time just before pupating. One caterpillar that escaped from the cage climbed about three-quarters of the way up my wall. It was just about to spin its silk pad when I found it. On the other hand, one homebody pupated on the passion flower stem just inches from where it had been feeding.

There are a number of fine-mesh rearing containers that are commercially available in various shapes and sizes, from small ones that can hold a potted plant or two up to greenhouse-sized cages into which a person can walk. Many butterfly gardeners, however, like to make their own rearing containers out of plastic or cardboard boxes.

Whichever type of rearing cage you use for your caterpillars, it should be well ventilated in order to prevent mold and bacteria from growing, and disease from spreading. Since excessive heat can kill eggs, caterpillars, and pupae, the cage should be kept out of direct sunlight. In order to avoid injury to butterflies when they emerge, be sure they have enough room to spread their wings; a suitable surface (such as a horizontal branch on a stick) from which to hang; and enough sunlight to perform their initial biological functions, such as drying and pumping up their wings. You should pay close attention to butterflies immediately before and just after they emerge, to make sure no mishaps occur.

Your rearing cage should prevent wandering caterpillars from escaping. If you cover the cage with netting, be sure the mesh is fine enough so that even the smallest caterpillars cannot crawl through the holes. The larvae of some species will wander off their foodplant in early instars as well as just before pupating, so keep a close eye on them to be sure they stay on or near the foodplant.

When changing the foodplant, be careful not to handle caterpillars excessively. Tiny caterpillars may be moved with a small paint brush. Let them crawl onto the brush, and then crawl off onto the new foodplant. Children love to handle caterpillars, but you should instruct youngsters to be careful with larvae. One of the pleasures of rearing is being able to feel the varied textures of larval skin and hair. I was amazed at how cool a caterpillar's skin feels. Comprised of chitin, it doesn't retain heat the way other body parts do.

Make sure to change the foodplant daily and empty the frass regularly. If you use a box as a rearing container, line the bottom with paper toweling to make this easier. To make sure the foodplant stays fresh and the caterpillars don't become desiccated, slightly dampen the paper toweling. In order to change the foodplant, just put the old leaves onto the new ones and the caterpillars will crawl onto them.

You could also cover some potted foodplant with nylon netting and attach the netting to the outside of the pot with a rubber band or a piece of string. Place a stick in the soil so that it supports the netting. If the stick has a few branches, the caterpillars will have a number of places to pupate.

One butterfly rearer gave me a setup that worked extremely well with the butterflies that I reared in my apartment. It consisted of a few simple items: an eight-inch by eight-inch by six-and-one-half-inch high cardboard box; a couple of glass jars; a two-foot stick with a number of horizontal and nearly vertical branches and protrusions; some soil; and the net part of a butterfly net. I placed both jars in the box. In one (which I filled almost to the top with water), I placed the stems of the foodplant into holes punched in the top. I placed the stick in the other and then filled it with dirt so the stick stood upright in the center. This gave the caterpillars something on which to pupate and also held up the netting, which I draped over the stick and secured to the outside of the box with a rubber band.

You should care properly for caterpillars. Be sure they have a constant supply of fresh foodplant. If you interrupt the supply of food when they're young, they may starve. When they're older, they may pupate early if they run out of food. The result may be a small or defective butterfly. Young caterpillars may not have large or strong enough jaws to gnaw on older leaves, so be sure to provide them with some young, tender leaves just in case. In general, you should provide caterpillars with a variety of young and mature leaves. Whatever the case, foodplants should always be fresh and succulent.

When using cut foodplants in water, make sure to cover any open areas around the stems. This will prevent caterpillars from falling or crawling down into the water and drowning. In order to make it easier for caterpillars to find the foodplant if they crawl off it, you could place some of the leaves so that they are flush against the bottom or sides of the cage.

Be careful not to disturb caterpillars when they're about to molt. Don't try to move them off a leaf at this time, because they attach themselves with silk to hold their skin as they pull out of it. If you move them off this spot, they might not get free of the old skin and they'll die. Newly molted larvae are very tender, so be extremely careful not to handle them or cause them to fall or be bumped by stems, the sides of boxes, or other objects.

Foodplants vary in terms of how long they'll remain fresh in water. Most will last a week or so and some will last over two weeks, but you shouldn't go much longer than this without replacing it. Many foodplants need to be replaced daily. In order to keep extra foodplant fresh, place it in tightly shut plastic bags and keep these bags in the refrigerator. You will have even better results if you place the stems in a jar filled with water, cover the jar with a plastic bag, and store the whole thing in the refrigerator. Foodplants should not be stored in the freezer. This is sure to wilt them when they defrost. By cutting across the bottom of foodplant stems, you will make it easier for the stem to absorb water. Making this cut at an angle will provide even more surface area for water absorption.

When collecting stems and leaves of foodplants in your neighborhood, avoid using plants from busy roadsides because they'll probably be covered with pollution from car exhaust. This could poison caterpillars, especially the smaller ones, whose bodies cannot withstand much contamination. Do not use foodplants that have been sprayed with insecticide or herbicide. To clean foodplants, rinse them in water. Let them dry before giving them to caterpillars.

Even if you watch caterpillars closely, you may get caught without enough foodplant on hand. Full-grown Anise Swallowtail larvae can finish off a few fennel sprays each day. One night I ran low on fennel, so I drove to a nearby patch. While clipping off the stems, I noticed a black and white blotch on one of the leaves. Though it resembled a bird dropping, experience told me that it was an early-instar Anise Swallowtail caterpillar. Searching the rest of the plant, I discovered two more young larvae. I brought all three home, along with more foodplant than I had originally intended to gather. This was an unexpected, yet rewarding turn of events. I had never located wild Anise Swallowtail larvae on my own; and now I had the prospect of seeing three more Anise Swallowtails emerge in my apartment.

Chrysalises are very fragile and should not be handled frequently or roughly. If you live in a place with low humidity, you may need to spray the pupae once a week with a fine mist. Be careful not to get them too damp, or they might develop mold.

When collecting chrysalises in the wild or handling them at home, make sure you don't turn them upside down from their natural position or disturb them in any way. Chrysalises collected in the wild should be taken with their stems. If this is not possible (for example, the chrysalis is attached to a fence), you can remove it by slowly and gently twisting it off its silk pad. Be careful not to squeeze the pupa too hard, or you might damage or fatally injure it. If you slice the silk pad close to the point of attachment, you may have better (and safer) results. You can attach the pupa to your own surface with a tiny drop of glue or, if there's enough silk on which to attach it, with some tape.

If a pupa is attached to a piece of wood with bark, slice a strip of the bark and bring the bark back to your rearing cage. This is especially useful with swallowtails, which attach themselves with a silken girdle as well as the pad. If you need to cut the girdle to obtain a pupa, do so and replace the girdle with a loop of thread. Tape the thread to the new surface so that the pupa remains at the same angle at which you found it.

Once, when rearing some Monarchs, my pupa-handling skills were put to the test. Two of the caterpillars pupated on branches of the stick I had provided, but one pupated on the netting that covered the cage. I wanted to photograph the pupae on the stick, so as gently and slowly as I could, I lifted the netting. It caught on a piece of branch, causing the chrysalis to fall. Fortunately, its silk pad unraveled and got caught on a tiny protrusion on one of the branches, breaking its fall. After cutting away the excess silk, I attached the pupa to an $8\frac{1}{2} \times 11$-inch piece of cardboard by placing a few narrow strips of masking tape over what was left of the silk pad. I placed the cardboard over a small box so the butterfly would have enough room when it emerged, but wouldn't be able to fly away. Four days later, a healthy butterfly emerged. When I released it, I felt very satisfied (and relieved) that it had made it safely to adulthood.

Indeed, perhaps the greatest reward of rearing butterflies comes when you bring a newly emerged butterfly outside and watch it fly off into the sky. Whether you release a butterfly in the city or in the country, the gratification is akin to watching a child go out into the world. It's a joyful feeling—the joy of watching the natural process in all of its majesty.

Atala (foreground) and Monarch (background)

CHAPTER 9

Conservation of Butterflies

In his *Audubon Society Handbook for Butterfly Watchers,* Robert Michael Pyle discusses a concept that he calls the "extinction of experience." This results when not only wholly endangered species but also local populations of creatures diminish under the pressures of human development. "Suppose a creature dies out within your 'radius of reach'— the area to which you have easy access," he states. "In some respects, it might as well be gone altogether, because you will not be able to see it as you could before." According to Pyle, this extinction of experience can snowball, causing people to be more isolated from, and less caring of nature. "On the other hand," he goes on, "the retention of wildlife in the cities and suburbs goes a long way toward maintaining the essential bond between people and nature that breeds a sense of stewardship and responsibility for the land and its life far beyond city limits."

As we have seen, butterfly gardeners experience and maintain this bond between people and nature. But the pressures on butterflies and other forms of wildlife continue to mount, even though people's attitudes about conserving butterflies and other insects have changed. "Once almost entirely neglected in favor of larger, furrier animals, butterflies and other beneficial insects under threat have gained much attention lately," Pyle states. "This change of attitude is coming none too quickly, and it is not at all certain that it has come in time. We are beginning to realize that, without great care, we could lose much of the world's precious butterfly resource."

Among the many causes for the decline of butterflies, the destruction of their habitat by human expansion is by far the greatest. Closely tied to their environment, butterflies are extremely sensitive to ecological changes. Thus, when a butterfly lives in a restricted area, the alteration of that area can threaten the butterfly's survival. If a butterfly is rare enough, this could cause its extinction. Some butterflies, such as the Xerces Blue of the San Francisco Peninsula, have already become extinct.

Not only rare and endangered butterflies are vulnerable. Many common species, especially in urban areas, have been declining. Habitat destruction, including land development, the draining of wetlands, and the conversion of diverse habitats into monocultures, causes most of the problem. Additional factors that contribute to the loss of butterflies include the use of pesticides and collecting. But except in cases where a butterfly is exceedingly rare and local, collecting has a minimal impact, primarily because butterflies have such a high reproductive rate. Many more butterflies fall victim to predation and bad weather than to collecting. A drought, a wildfire, a cold or hot spell, or a flood can wipe out an entire butterfly colony, either by destroying their foodplant or the butterflies themselves.

It is important, therefore, to protect the habitats of butterflies, and in this respect, butterfly gardeners can play a useful role. If you establish a colony of butterflies in your yard, this will help to increase their numbers in the neighborhood. You could also rear butterflies indoors from the egg through the adult stage and then release them. This protects them from predators and the weather. But when released, they must find suitable habitat, or perish. Hence the garden's value. Not everyone has the opportunity to provide a butterfly garden for an endangered species, but if a butterfly is somewhat rare in your area, you could help it out. Even common butterflies need all the help they can get. While a few species such as the Cabbage White and Orange Sulphur have adapted well to human environments, most need special consideration to remain prolific.

In the case of the Atala butterfly, once thought to be extinct in southeastern Florida, suburban gardeners have adopted the butterfly's foodplant, a species of cycad called the Coontie, as part of their landscaping designs, and the Atala has made a comeback.

Garden clubs have been influential in promoting butterfly conservation and education among their members. One shining example of this is the collaboration between National Garden Clubs and the National Fund for the U.S. Botanic Garden (now called the Friends of the U.S.

Atala

Botanic Garden). Over a number of years, these organizations conducted a fundraising campaign to establish a butterfly garden (now called the Pollinator Garden) at the United States Botanic Garden in Washington, DC, and lo and behold, they succeeded.

The North American Butterfly Association operates the National Butterfly Center in Mission, Texas, where more than 240 species of butterflies have been seen amid the foodplants and nectar sources that have been planted especially for these flying wonders on this preserve that is open to the public. The NABA also has a butterfly garden and habitat program that encourages people to grow foodplants and nectar sources for butterflies. This group conducts butterfly counts that are held at various times of the year, especially on the Fourth of July. These counts contribute valuable information about the distribution and abundance of butterflies in numerous regions of the United States, Canada, and Mexico.

In recent years, some federally endangered butterflies have been helped along by interested individuals and institutions, and their populations have increased. For example, Los Angeles World Airports manages a preserve for the El Segundo Blue, which only survives in a few patches of buckwheat by the Pacific Ocean. Habitat restoration has played a large role in saving this butterfly from extinction. In the nearby Ballona Wetlands, the El Segundo Blue established itself in a small area where non-native plants were removed and the native coastal buckwheat was encouraged to grow.

Meanwhile, the Palos Verdes Blue, once thought to be extinct, has been the beneficiary of a recovery program that includes captive breeding and release of the butterflies, and a restoration of its habitat of locoweed and deerweed foodplants. This has resulted in an increase in this butterfly's population as well.

At the Albany Pine Brush Preserve in New York State, a combination of captive rearing and habitat restoration of these ancient pine barrens has resulted in a recovery of the endangered Karner Blue. This butterfly feeds on wild lupine, which thrives in areas that are periodically disturbed. At the preserve, habitat areas as well as butterfly numbers have grown substantially for this species, which also occurs in isolated populations in a number of states in the Midwest.

Perhaps our most iconic butterfly, the Monarch, has suffered population declines in recent years due to the removal of its milkweed foodplant from the prairies of North America in favor of herbicide-resistant corn and soybean crops; commercial development; and loss of habitat in its overwintering grounds in Mexico. Monarch Watch, an organization based at the University of Kansas, encourages people to plant milkweeds and nectar sources in home gardens, schools, and parks as part of its "Monarch Waystation" program designed to offer refuges for Monarchs along their migration route. The idea is to provide foodplants for the Monarchs to produce successive generations in their spring and summer breeding areas, and to have nectar sources available for the butterflies while they are on their southward migration in the fall.

When we think of endangered and threatened species, we often think of larger animals like the California condor, the whooping crane, and the grizzly bear. The attitude that insects are worthy of the same protection as large animals has been a relatively recent phenomenon, perhaps because we tend to think of insects as pests. However, relatively few insects compete with humans, and most, including almost all butterflies, are beneficial.

Among many reasons, butterflies should be protected for their aesthetic value. Butterfly gardeners know this as well as anyone. Most people would find it difficult to imagine a world without the beauty of butterflies. And yet, unique species like the Xerces Blue have been taken from us forever, and other butterflies face the same fate. When I see an illustration or photograph of an extinct butterfly, I feel a sense of frustration and emptiness as I realize that I'll never be able to see a live one.

Butterflies serve an important role in the food chain. And, as we've discussed, they pollinate many flowers when they take nectar. They also represent a valuable scientific and educational resource. Many medical discoveries have resulted from research performed on the genes and other biological characteristics of insects, including butterflies. Rare butterflies, restricted to small areas, furnish subjects for genetic research analyzing variations in wing colors, fertility, population dynamics, and aspects of evolution. The Xerces Blue, with its variable spots, would have been perfect for this. When butterflies disappear, so do the opportunities to study unique biological systems.

Perhaps the most important benefit we can get from butterflies is their service as ecological indicators. If a butterfly is endangered, this

Monarch

means that the habitat in which it lives is at risk, along with the other insects, plants, and vertebrates that occur within it. Endangered butterflies therefore serve as extremely delicate barometers of the natural conditions in these areas. A large animal with a wide range wouldn't be as useful for pinpointing a trouble spot. Ironically, while one would think that minute butterflies living in tiny colonies would be virtually impossible to protect, it is often because they live in such small spaces that they are passed over and escape destruction. But unless positive steps ensure their long-term protection, they may eventually succumb to the fate of the Xerces Blue: extinction through ignorance.

In contrast, wider-ranging butterflies such as the Monarch face a different danger—the wholesale alteration of the countryside. The decline of many butterflies indicates the extent to which our environment has been robbed of its natural features. We can read this as a warning of our own degree of danger. It could be, then, that by protecting butterflies, we are in fact taking steps toward our own survival.

Left to right: Queen, Common Buckeye, and Monarch

Fifty North American Garden Butterflies

The following list contains information about fifty species of butterflies that breed regularly in the United States and Canada. Depending on the region in which you live, you may have a good chance of attracting any of these butterflies to your garden. The ranges refer to the contiguous United States.

SWALLOWTAILS

(*Papilionidae*)

Anise Swallowtail

(*Papilio zelicaon*)

RANGE: Most of western U.S.

FOODPLANT: Various members of the carrot family (Umbelliferae), including fennel (*Foeniculum vulgare*), carrots, parsley, cow parsnip (*Heracleum maximum*), seaside angelica (*Angelica lucida*); citrus trees.

NECTAR PREFERENCES: Lomatium, penstemon, mint, zinnia, lantana, butterfly bush, coltsfoot.

ON WING: Spring to fall, year-round in South.

BROODS: One, two, or multiple broods.

HIBERNATES AS: Chrysalis.

HABITATS: Open areas, roadsides, mountains, deserts, shorelines.

SPECIAL FEATURES: Males congregate on hilltops and at mud puddles. Males also patrol, searching for females. Easy to rear.

Black Swallowtail

(*Papilio polyxenes*)

RANGE: Eastern U.S. to Rocky Mountains; Arizona, New Mexico.

FOODPLANT: Various members of the carrot family (Umbelliferae), including Queen Anne's lace (*Daucus carota*), cultivated carrot, celery, parsley, parsnip, dill, caraway; members of the citrus family (Rutaceae), including rue (*Ruta graveolens*), Texas turpentine broom (*Thamnosma texana*).

NECTAR PREFERENCES: Milkweed, thistle, phlox, clover, alfalfa, Queen Anne's lace, purple loosestrife.

ON WING: February–November, depending on latitude.

BROODS: Two in North, three in South.

HIBERNATES AS: Chrysalis.

HABITATS: Open fields, meadows, roadsides, streamsides.

SPECIAL FEATURES: Especially fond of vegetable gardens. Female mimics Pipevine Swallowtail. Newly emerged males visit damp areas. Males perch and patrol, searching for females.

Eastern Tiger Swallowtail

(*Papilio glaucus*)

RANGE: Entire U.S. east of Rockies.

FOODPLANT: Cherry (*Prunus*), ash (*Fraxinus*), birch (*Betula*), aspen, cottonwood (*Populus*), tulip tree (*Liriodendron tulipifera*), willow (*Salix*), sweet bay (*Magnolia virginiana*), hop tree (*Ptelea trifoliata*), spicebush (*Lindera benzoin*), lilac (*Syringa vulgaris*), American hornbeam (*Carpinus caroliniana*).

NECTAR PREFERENCES: Butterfly bush, thistle, milkweed, Japanese honeysuckle, phlox, Joe-Pye weed, clover, lilac, abelia, buttonbush, bee balm, ironweed, sunflower, dandelion.

ON WING: February-November, depending on latitude.

BROODS: One-three.

HIBERNATES AS: Chrysalis.

HABITATS: Woodlands, streamsides, roadsides, orchards, savannahs, towns.

SPECIAL FEATURES: Dark female form mimics Pipevine Swallowtail. High flier, but often descends into gardens, especially ovipositing females. Adults sometimes nectar in groups. Newly emerged males visit mud puddles and streamsides, and patrol, searching for females.

Giant Swallowtail

(*Papilio cresphontes*)

RANGE: Most of U.S., except extreme North.

FOODPLANT: Various citrus trees (Rutaceae), including orange trees, common prickly-ash (*Zanthoxylum americanum*), Hercules-club (*Z. clava-herculis*), common hoptree (*Ptelea trifoliate*), rue (*Ruta graveolens*), sea amyris (*Amyris elemifera*).

NECTAR PREFERENCES: Lantana, Japanese honeysuckle, milkweed, lilac, goldenrod, orange blossom, azalea, dame's rocket, bougainvillea, bouncing bet.

ON WING: May-September in North, year-round in far South.

BROODS: Two in North, three in South.

HIBERNATES AS: Chrysalis.

HABITATS: Open woodlands, forest edges, roadsides, citrus groves, streamsides.

SPECIAL FEATURES: This species is the largest butterfly in North America. High flier, but often descends into gardens, especially ovipositing females. Caterpillar is called the "Orange Dog," and may become plentiful in citrus groves. Males often visit moist ground, and patrol areas, searching for females.

Old World Swallowtail

(*Papilio machaon*)

RANGE: Montana, western U.S.

FOODPLANT: Dragon wormwood (*Artemisia dracunculus*).

NECTAR PREFERENCES: Penstemon, mint, *Senecio*.

ON WING: May–September.

BROODS: Two.

HIBERNATES AS: Chrysalis.

HABITATS: Mountains.

SPECIAL FEATURES: Good for gardeners at higher elevations. The Northwest variety (*P.m. oregonius*) is the state insect of Oregon.

Pipevine Swallowtail

(*Battus philenor*)

RANGE: Most of U.S.

FOODPLANT: Various species of pipevine, including Dutchman's pipe (*Aristolochia durior*), Virginia snakeroot (*A. serpentaria*), *A. californica* and *A. longiflora*.

NECTAR PREFERENCES: Thistle, lilac, honeysuckle, milkweed, butterfly bush, azalea, orchid, phlox, clover, bergamot, viper's bugloss, dame's rocket, teasel, petunia, fruit tree blossoms.

ON WING: January–November, depending on latitude.

BROODS: Two in North, three in South.

HIBERNATES AS: Chrysalis.

HABITATS: Open forests, fields, roadsides, meadows.

SPECIAL FEATURES: Distasteful to birds. Mimicked by the palatable female Black Swallowtail, female Ozark Swallowtail, dark female Eastern Tiger Swallowtail, Spicebush Swallowtail, Red-spotted Admiral, and female Diana Fritillary. Males patrol areas, searching for females.

Spicebush Swallowtail

(*Papilio troilus*)

RANGE: Most of U.S. east of Rockies.

FOODPLANT: Spicebush (*Lindera benzoin*), sassafras (*Sassafras albidum*), tulip tree (*Liriodendron tulipifera*), sweet bay (*Magnolia virginiana*), common prickly ash (*Zanthoxylum americanum*), bay (*Persea*).

NECTAR PREFERENCES: Honeysuckle, thistle, jewelweed, milkweed, clover, Joe-Pye weed, lantana, azalea, dogbane, sweet pepperbush, mimosa.

ON WING: Mid-April to mid-October, depending on latitude.

BROODS: Two in North, three in South.

HIBERNATES AS: Chrysalis.

HABITATS: Woodlands, fields, meadows, streamsides, pine barrens.

SPECIAL FEATURES: Mimics the Pipevine Swallowtail. Newly emerged males visit mud puddles and streamsides, patrol open areas.

Western Tiger Swallowtail

(*Papilio rutulus*)

RANGE: Most of western U.S.

FOODPLANT: Alder (*Alnus*), aspen, poplar (*Populus*), willow (*Salix*), sycamore (*Platanus*).

NECTAR PREFERENCES: Butterfly bush, thistle, milkweed, lilac, phlox, teasel, glossy abelia, mint, blackberry, lilies, agapanthus (lily-of-the-Nile), hibiscus, lantana.

ON WING: February–July, depending on latitude.

BROODS: One-three.

HIBERNATES AS: Chrysalis.

HABITATS: Streamsides, roadsides, canyons, parks, townscapes.

SPECIAL FEATURES: Possibly the most visible western butterfly. Males visit mud puddles and streamsides, and establish territories. Caterpillar, with its big eyespots, resembles a green snake.

WHITES AND SULPHURS

(*Pieridae*)

Cabbage White

(*Pieris rapae*)

RANGE: Entire U.S.

FOODPLANT: Various members of the mustard family (Cruciferae), including cabbage, collards, broccoli, nasturtium (*Tropaeolum*), winter cress (*Barbarea*), mustard (*Brassica*), peppergrass (*Lepidium*); members of the caper family (Capparidaceae).

NECTAR PREFERENCES: Mustard, winter cress, arabis, aubrieta, dandelion, red clover, dogbane, aster, mint, self-heal wild bergamot, hedge-nettle, milkweed, wild oregano, cinquefoil, bristly ox tongue, lantana.

ON WING: Early spring to late fall in North, year-round in far South.

BROODS: Three in North, seven or eight in South.

HIBERNATES AS: Chrysalis.

HABITATS: Open woodlands, forest edges, agricultural fields, plains, urban waste places.

SPECIAL FEATURES: Probably the most widespread butterfly in North America. Especially fond of vegetable gardens. Newly emerged males visit moist ground and streamsides. Not a native; introduced to Canada in the 19th Century. Sometimes pestiferous, but often valuable as the only butterfly around.

California Dogface

(Colias eurydice)

RANGE: California, W. Arizona.

FOODPLANT: False indigo (*Amerpha*), clover (*Trifolium*), indigo bush (*Dalea*).

NECTAR PREFERENCES: Thistle, blue dicks, and its own foodplants.

ON WING: Spring to fall.

BROODS: Two.

HIBERNATES AS: Chrysalis.

HABITATS: Mountains, forest clearings, foothills.

SPECIAL FEATURES: "Dog's face" pattern adorns upperside of each forewing. Designated as California's official state insect. Males exhibit brilliant purplish sheen, lacking in the Southern Dogface.

Checkered White

(Pontia protodice)

RANGE: Most of U.S., absent from Northwest.

FOODPLANT: Various members of the mustard family (Cruciferae), including wild peppergrass (*Lepidium*), shepherd's purse

(*Capsella bursa-pastoris*), winter cress (*Barbarea* vulgaris); bee plant (*Cleome*).

NECTAR PREFERENCES: Hedge mustard, winter cress, milkweed, aster, centaury, spreading dogbane, salt heliotrope.

ON WING: March-November, depending on latitude; year-round in some areas of California.

BROODS: Three in North, four in South.

HIBERNATES AS: Chrysalis.

HABITATS: Open areas, agricultural fields, roadsides, sandy places.

SPECIAL FEATURES: Males patrol in search of females. A good butterfly for altered landscapes and urban vacant lots; can be extremely abundant.

Cloudless Sulphur

(*Phoebis sennae*)

RANGE: Most of southern and eastern U.S., except extreme North.

FOODPLANT: Senna (*Cassia*), partridge pea (*Chamaecrista cinerea*), clover (*Trifolium*).

NECTAR PREFERENCES: Lantana, geranium, hibiscus, cardinal flower, bougainvillea, morning glory, daisy, cordia, thistle.

ON WING: June-September, year-round in far South.

BROODS: Two in North, three in South.

HIBERNATES AS: Cannot overwinter in cold climates.

HABITATS: Open areas, roadsides, fields, beaches, streamsides.

SPECIAL FEATURES: Large numbers emigrate outward from dense populations, especially in autumn. Sometimes individuals roost communally. It wanders widely, leading this spectacular, clear yellow species to be seen far out of its normal breeding range. Caterpillar constructs nest from silk and leaves of host plant, and hides in it during the day.

Clouded Sulphur

(*Colias philodice*)

RANGE: Entire U.S., except most of Florida.

FOODPLANT: Various members of the pea family (Leguminosae), including white clover (*Trifolium repens*), other clovers (*Trifolium*), trefoil (*Lotus*), vetch (*Vicia*), alfalfa (*Medicago*), white sweet clover (*Melilotus alba*).

NECTAR PREFERENCES: Clover, goldenrod, dandelion, aster, tickseed sunflower, knapweed, milkweed, phlox, dogbane, winter cress.

ON WING: March–December, according to location.

BROODS: Three–five, depending on latitude.

HIBERNATES AS: Chrysalis.

HABITATS: Open areas, agricultural fields, roadsides, meadows.

SPECIAL FEATURES: Known as the Mud Puddle Butterfly, because large groups of males congregate at mud puddles. Especially fond of vegetable gardens and lawns. Very easy to rear.

Falcate Orangetip

(*Anthocharis midea*)

RANGE: Eastern U.S. from Massachusetts to Wisconsin, south to Georgia, Louisiana, and central Texas.

FOODPLANT: Various members of the mustard family (Cruciferae), including rock cress (*Arabis*), bitter cress (*Cardamine*), winter cress (*Barbarea*), hedge mustard (*Sisymbrium*), shepherd's purse (*Capsella bursa-pastoris*), cut-leaved toothwort (*Centaria laciniata*).

NECTAR PREFERENCES: Cresses, peppergrass, mustard, wild strawberry, violet, toothwort, chickweed, spring-beauty, wild plum.

ON WING: March–June.

BROODS: One in North, two in South.

HIBERNATES AS: Chrysalis.

HABITATS: Open woodlands, streamsides, pine barrens, roadsides.

SPECIAL FEATURES: Spring butterfly. Low-flying. Will fly on cloudy days. Males patrol areas, searching for females, and sometimes congregate on hilltops.

Orange Sulphur

(*Colias eurytheme*)

RANGE: Entire U.S.

FOODPLANT: Various members of the pea family (Leguminosae), including alfalfa (*Medicago sativa*), white clover (*Trifolium repens*), white sweet clover (*Melilotus alba*), vetch (*Vicia*), crown vetch (*Coronilla*), wild indigo (*Baptisia*).

NECTAR PREFERENCES: Alfalfa, clover, thistle, aster, goldenrod, coreopsis, tickseed sunflower, rabbitbrush, dandelion, salt heliotrope, milkweed, winter cress, dogbane, osier dogwood.

ON WING: March–December, depending on latitude.

BROODS: Three–five.

HIBERNATES AS: Chrysalis.

HABITATS: Open areas, alfalfa fields.

SPECIAL FEATURES: Also called the Alfalfa Butterfly, because of its caterpillars' fondness for alfalfa. Adults often roost in small groups. Newly emerged males visit moist ground and streamsides. Can be enormously abundant in alfalfa fields and clover meadows.

Sara Orangetip

(*Anthocharis sara*)

RANGE: Much of U.S. from Rockies west.

FOODPLANT: Various members of the mustard family (Cruciferae), including rock cress (*Arabis*), mustard (*Brassica*), winter cress (*Barbarea*), hedge mustard (*Sisymbrium officinale*).

NECTAR PREFERENCES: Dandelion, strawberry, bitter cherry, monkey flower, blue dicks.

ON WING: February–July, according to altitude and latitude.

BROODS: One or two.

HABITATS: Woodlands, mountains, deserts, meadows, streamsides, fields.

SPECIAL FEATURES: Most abundant in spring. Low-flying and an avid drinker of nectar, thus highly observable. Brilliant on the wing. Orange wingtips and green marbling on underside are very striking.

Sleepy Orange

(*Eurema nicippe*)

RANGE: Southern and southwestern U.S., most of eastern U.S. except extreme North.

FOODPLANT: Various members of the pea family (Leguminosae), including senna (*Cassia*), clover (*Trifolium*).

NECTAR PREFERENCES: Beggar-ticks, other composites.

ON WING: March–November, depending on latitude; year-round in far South.

BROODS: Two-five.

HIBERNATES AS: Cannot overwinter in cold climates.

HABITATS: Forest edges, fields, meadows, roadsides, streamsides.

SPECIAL FEATURES: Emigrates northward, filling in much of the country with summer generations that die off in autumn. Males puddle and patrol.

Southern Dogface

(*Colias cesonia*)

RANGE: Most of southern U.S., Midwest; occasionally Northeast.

FOODPLANT: Various members of the pea family (Leguminosae), including false indigo (*Amphora*), clover (*Trifolium*), indigo bush (*Dalea*), prairie clover (*Pentalostemon*), soybean (*Glycine*).

NECTAR PREFERENCES: Alfalfa, coreopsis, *Houstonia*, verbena.

ON WING: Mid to late-summer in North, almost year-round in South.

BROODS: Three.

HIBERNATES AS: Chrysalis or adult.

HABITATS: Open woodlands, deserts, prairies.

SPECIAL FEATURES: Note "dog's face" on upperside of each forewing. Butterfly emigrates northward. Newly emerged males visit puddles and patrol for females.

GOSSAMER-WING BUTTERFLIES

(*Lycaenidae*)

Boisduval's blue

(*Plebejus icarioides*)

RANGE: Most of western U.S.

FOODPLANT: Various species of lupine (*Lupinus*).

NECTAR PREFERENCES: Lupine, milkweed, various composites.

ON WING: April–August, the lower the altitude and farther south, the earlier.

BROODS: One.

HIBERNATES AS: Half-grown caterpillar.

HABITATS: Meadows, streamsides, mountains, roadsides.

SPECIAL FEATURES: Always found near lupines. Visits puddles and flowers. Larvae are tended by ants. Best suited to a large western garden little changed from native grasslands.

Brown Elfin

(*Callophrys augustinus*)

RANGE: Most of U.S.

FOODPLANT: Various members of the heath family (*Ericaceae*) in East, including blueberry (*Vaccinium*), azalea (*Rhododendron*), sugar huckleberry (*Vaccinium vacillans*), leatherleaf (*Chamaedaphne*), bearberry (*Arctostaphylos uva-ursi*), huckleberry (*Gaylussacia*), Labrador tea (*Ledum groenlandicum*); in West, dodder (*Cuscata*), California lilac (*Ceanothus*), salal (*Gaultheria*), apple (*Malus*), madrone (*Arbutus*).

NECTAR PREFERENCES: Winter cress, blueberry, bitter cherry, wild buckwheat, footsteps of spring, willow, bearberry, wild plum, bitterbrush.

ON WING: April–June.

BROODS: One.

HIBERNATES AS: Chrysalis.

HABITATS: Forest edges, open woodlands, acid bogs, pine barrens.

SPECIAL FEATURES: Spring butterfly, in general. Visits moist ground and streamsides. Males perch and dart out after females and other passing objects. Survives in urban settings where hosts abound.

Eastern Pygmy-Blue

(*Brephidium isophthalma*)

RANGE: Eastern U.S. coast from South Carolina to Florida, Louisiana, and sometimes Texas.

FOODPLANT: Glasswort (*Salicornia*), saltwort (*Batis*).

NECTAR PREFERENCES: Saltwort, lippia, palmetto.

ON WING: February–September, year-round in far South.

BROODS: Multiple.

HIBERNATES AS: Perhaps unable to overwinter in the North.

HABITATS: Saltwater areas, tidal flats.

SPECIAL FEATURES: Smallest eastern butterfly. Coastal species. Males patrol near foodplant, searching for females.

Gray Hairstreak

(*Strymon melinus*)

RANGE: Entire U.S.

FOODPLANT: Various plants in many families; favorites are members of the pea (Leguminosae) and mallow (Malvaceae) families, including clover (*Trifolium*), mallow (*Malva*), vetch (*Vicia*), beans (*Phaseolus*), tick-trefoil (*Desmodium*), bush clover (*Lespedeza*), cotton (*Gossypium*), hibiscus (*Hibiscus*); also corn (*Zea mays*), mint (*Lamiacea*), oak (*Quercus*), strawberry (*Fragaria*), hawthorn (*Crataegus*), and hops (*Humulus*).

NECTAR PREFERENCES: Milkweed, white sweet clover, winter cress, Cape plumbago, goldenrod, yellow bee plant, mint, dogbane, bitterbrush, Queen Anne's lace, tick-trefoil, sweet pea.

ON WING: April–October, earlier in the far South.

BROODS: Two-four.

HIBERNATES AS: Chrysalis.

HABITATS: Open areas, fields, roadsides, chaparral, open forests.

SPECIAL FEATURES: One of our most common and omnivorous species. Emigrates widely. Males exhibit territorial behavior, often perch on shrubs and small trees and dart out after potential females and interloping males.

Marine Blue

(*Leptotes marina*)

RANGE: Most of western U.S.

FOODPLANT: Various members of the pea family (Leguminosae), including alfalfa (*Medicago sativa*), false indigo (*Amorpha*), beans (*Phaseolus*), sweet pea (*Lathyrus odoratus*), locoweed (*Astragalus*); also leadwort (*Plumbago*), wisteria (*Wisteria*).

NECTAR PREFERENCES: Cape plumbago, wild buckwheat, oleander, Mexican fire plant, salt heliotrope, *Haplopappus*.

ON WING: Year-round in South, emigrates north in summer.

BROODS: Multiple.

HIBERNATES AS: Overwinters in any stage in frost-free zones.

HABITATS: Open areas, streamsides, plains, foothills.

SPECIAL FEATURES: Emigrates northward in summer, dies off in the fall. Visits moist spots and follows watercourses in its wanderings.

Silvery Blue

(*Glaucopsyche lygdamus*)

RANGE: Most of U.S.

FOODPLANT: Various members of the pea family (Leguminosae), including wild pea (*Lathyrus*), vetch (*Vicia*), lupine (*Lupinus*), white sweet clover (*Melilotus alba*), deer weed (*Lotus scoparius*), locoweed (*Astragalus*).

NECTAR PREFERENCES: Coneflower and other composites, lomatium, bitter cherry, lupine.

ON WING: March-July, depending on latitude and altitude.

BROODS: One.

HIBERNATES AS: Chrysalis.

HABITATS: Open forests, fields, streamsides, prairies, mountain meadows, roadside seeps.

SPECIAL FEATURES: Spring butterfly that can be induced into the garden. Visits puddles and patrols near foodplant. Larvae are tended by ants, which provide protection in return for honeydew.

Spring Azure

(*Celastrina ladon*)

RANGE: Entire U.S.

FOODPLANT: Dogwood (*Cornus*), ceanothus (*Ceanothus*), viburnum (*Viburnum*), cherry (*Prunus*), sumac (*Rhus*), meadowsweet (*Spiraea salicifolia*), blueberry (*Vaccinium*), black snakeroot (*Cimicifuga racemosa*), wingstem (*Actinomeris alternifolia*).

NECTAR PREFERENCES: Holly, privet, ceanothus, ivy, rock cress, winter cress, escallonia, blackberry, cotoneaster, milkweed, forget-me-not, dogbane, willow, spicebush, coltsfoot, dandelion, violet, cherry.

ON WING: January-October, depending on latitude.

BROODS: Usually one in North, two or three farther south.

HIBERNATES AS: Chrysalis.

HABITATS: Open woodlands, fields, roadsides, freshwater marshes, forest edges, townscapes.

SPECIAL FEATURES: Spring butterfly, in general. Males visit damp spots and droppings, and patrol and sometimes perch and dart out after females. A very good garden habitué.

Western Pygmy-Blue

(*Brephidium exile*)

RANGE: Most of western U.S.

FOODPLANT: Various members of the goosefoot family (Chenopodiaceae), including pigweed (*Chenopodium*), saltbush (*Atriplex*), pickleweed (*Salicornia ambigua*).

NECTAR PREFERENCES: Mexican fire plant, pigweed, salt heliotrope.

ON WING: Spring–fall, year-round in far South.

BROODS: Multiple.

HIBERNATES AS: May emigrate into cold areas in spring.

HABITATS: Disturbed areas, alkaline places, marshes.

SPECIAL FEATURES: Smallest western butterfly. Emigrates widely, so unpredictable in gardens. Larvae are tended by ants.

BRUSH-FOOTED BUTTERFLIES

(*Nymphalidae*)

American Lady

(*Vanessa virginiensis*)

RANGE: Entire U.S., but much scarcer in the West than in the East.

FOODPLANT: Various species of everlasting, including pearly everlasting (*Anaphalis margaritacea*), sweet everlasting (*Gnaphalium obtusifolium*), plantain-leaved pussy toes (*Antennaria plantaginifolia*); other members of the daisy family (Compositae), including burdock (*Arctium*), ironweed (*Vernonia*), wormwood (*Artemisia*).

NECTAR PREFERENCES: Composites such as thistle, knapweed, common yarrow, goldenrod, aster, marigold, and zinnia; also milkweed, butterfly bush, mallow, buttonbush, red clover, vetch, mint, self-heal, privet, scabiosa, dogbane, sweet pepperbush, winter cress, salt heliotrope.

ON WING: May–November, year-round in far South.

BROODS: Two-four.

HIBERNATES AS: Adult or chrysalis.

HABITATS: Open areas, meadows, streamsides.

SPECIAL FEATURES: Adults may be able to overwinter in North. Exhibits some emigratory behavior. Butterfly often basks on bare ground. Visits moist spots. Eggs laid singly. Caterpillar constructs nest of silk, leaves, and other plant material. Large "eyespots" distinguish it from other ladies.

Common Buckeye

(*Junonia coenia*)

RANGE: Southern U.S., spreading northward in summer.

FOODPLANT: Various members of the snapdragon family (Scrophulariaceae), including snapdragon (*Antirrhinum*), toad-flax (*Linaria*), false foxglove (*Aureolaria*), monkey flower (*Mimulus*), figwort (*Scrophularia*); plantain (*Plantago*); verbena (*Verbena*); ruellia (*Ruellia nodiflora*).

NECTAR PREFERENCES: Composites such as aster, knapweed, gumweed, tickseed sunflower, chicory, and coreopsis; also plantain, wild buckwheat, peppermint, dogbane, milkweed.

ON WING: March–October, year-round in far South.

BROODS: Two–four.

HIBERNATES AS: Probably unable to hibernate in cold areas.

HABITATS: Open areas, meadows, fields, roadsides, shorelines.

SPECIAL FEATURES: Emigrates northward in spring, broadly in fall. Fond of basking on bare ground and visiting mud puddles. Exhibits territorial behavior. Males perch and patrol, searching for females. Impermanent garden guests, except in the South.

Common Wood-Nymph

(*Cercyonis pegala*)

RANGE: Most of U.S., except southern Florida, northern Maine, and northwest coast.

FOODPLANT: Various species of grasses (Poaceae).

NECTAR PREFERENCES: Rotting fruit, sap, flowers such as alfalfa, purple coneflower, mint, spiraea, sunflower, fleabane, penstemon, virgin's-bower, ironweed.

ON WING: June–September.

BROODS: One.

HIBERNATES AS: Newly hatched caterpillar.

HABITATS: Woodsides, meadows, grasslands, marshes, roadsides.

SPECIAL FEATURES: Often lands on tree trunks. Males patrol glades, searching for females. Like other satyrs, flight is not strong but expert as the butterfly flits among grassblades. An unmowed grassy meadow is essential if you want wood-nymphs around your garden.

Eastern Comma

(*Polygonia comma*)

RANGE: Entire U.S. from Great Plains east.

FOODPLANT: Hops (*Humulus*), nettle (*Urtica*), false nettle (*Boehmeria cylindrica*), wood nettle (*Laportea canadensis*), elm (*Ulmus*).

NECTAR PREFERENCES: Rotting fruit, sap, flowers such as butterfly bush, ivy, Michaelmas daisy, hebe, showy stonecrop, dandelion.

ON WING: Spring–fall.

BROODS: Two in North, three in South.

HIBERNATES AS: Adult.

HABITATS: Open woodlands, streamsides, roadsides.

SPECIAL FEATURES: Silvery "comma" mark on underside of each hindwing. Butterfly also called the Hop Merchant, because of its caterpillars' fondness for hops. Caterpillar constructs a shelter from a leaf of the foodplant. Habits similar to Question Mark; both have early and late season forms.

Great Spangled Fritillary

(*Speyeria cybele*)

RANGE: Most of U.S., except extreme Southeast.

FOODPLANT: Various species of violet (Viola).

NECTAR PREFERENCES: Composites such as thistle, Joe-Pye weed, ironweed, black-eyed Susan, and purple coneflower; also cardinal flower, bergamot, red clover, vetch, milkweed, verbena, mountain laurel, New Jersey tea.

ON WING: June-September.

BROODS: One.

HIBERNATES AS: Newly hatched caterpillar.

HABITATS: Open areas, woodlands, moist meadows, roadsides.

SPECIAL FEATURES: The largest fritillary. Especially fond of thistles. Floats with a slow, gradual flight when relaxed and pauses to nectar at length, affording excellent photographic opportunities.

Gulf Fritillary

(*Agraulis vanillae*)

RANGE: Southern U.S., visiting middle latitudes in summer.

FOODPLANT: Various species of passion flower (*Passiflora*).

NECTAR PREFERENCES: Lantana, composites such as beggar-ticks and thistle; also passion flower, cordia.

ON WING: Early spring to winter, year-round in far South.

BROODS: Multiple.

HIBERNATES AS: Cannot overwinter where frost occurs.

HABITATS: Open areas, fields, forest edges, pastures, canyons.

SPECIAL FEATURES: Emigrates north. Fast-flying. Males patrol in search of females. A very suitable butterfly for southern cities, easy to rear and habituate to gardens. A longwing rather than a true fritillary, yet silver-spotted and spectacular.

Hackberry Emperor

(*Asterocampa celtis*)

RANGE: Most of U.S. east of the Dakotas, and Arizona.

FOODPLANT: Various species of hackberry (*Celtis*).

NECTAR PREFERENCES: Rotting fruit, sap, dung, carrion, flowers such as milkweed.

ON WING: May–October, depending on location.

BROODS: One or two in North, three in South.

HIBERNATES AS: Egg or caterpillar.

HABITATS: Woodlands, forest edges, watercourses, roadsides, parks, cemeteries, suburbs.

SPECIAL FEATURES: Often perches on hackberry trees or other posts such as signs, headstones, or persons standing still. Can become extremely numerous. Easily lured to overripe bananas, and reared from the attractive green caterpillars and chrysalises. Another hackberry feeder, the Tawny Emperor (*A. clyton*), may be more common in your area.

Milbert's Tortoiseshell

(*Nymphalis milberti*)
RANGE: Northern U.S., occasionally in South.
FOODPLANT: Nettle (*Urtica*).

NECTAR PREFERENCES: Rotting fruit, sap, composites such as thistle, sneezeweed, Gloriosa daisy, Shasta daisy, Michaelmas daisy, ox-eye daisy, goldenrod, aster, marigold, and ageratum; also butterfly bush, lilac, stonecrop, showy stonecrop, rock cress, Siberian wallflower.

ON WING: March–November.

BROODS: Two-three.

HIBERNATES AS: Adult.

HABITATS: Woodlands, forest edges, fields, meadows, riversides, roadsides.

SPECIAL FEATURES: Appears in early spring, often pale and tattered after hibernating in a hollow tree or outbuilding. May take wing on sunny days in midwinter. Fresh, colorful new individuals come out in early summer. One of the best all-round garden butterflies.

Monarch

(*Danaus plexippus*)

RANGE: Entire U.S. except extreme Northwest.

FOODPLANT: Various species of milkweed (*Asclepias*); reported on dogbane (*Apocynum*).

NECTAR PREFERENCES: Milkweed, butterfly bush, composites such as goldenrod, beggar-ticks, tickseed sunflower, Joe-Pye weed, thistle, ironweed, gayfeather, Mexican sunflower, and cosmos; also dogbane, teasel, glossy abelia, lilac, buttonbush, lantana, mallow, various mints.

ON WING: Spring to fall over most of range, fall to spring in overwintering areas.

BROODS: Two-four in North, four-six or more in South.

HIBERNATES AS: None. Adult migrates to Mexico or California to overwinter in a few small sites.

HABITATS: Open areas, meadows, fields, roadsides, marshes.

SPECIAL FEATURES: Only butterfly to migrate north and south each year. Often roosts in large groups during migration. Overwinters in large congregations on trees. Distasteful to predators due to toxic milkweed hosts; mimicked by the palatable Viceroy. Our best-known and most beloved garden insect, virtually our national butterfly.

Mourning Cloak

(*Nymphalis antiopa*)

RANGE: Entire U.S.

FOODPLANT: Willow (*Salix*), elm (*Ulmus*), poplar, aspen, cottonwood (*Populus*), birch (*Betula*), hackberry (*Celtis*).

NECTAR PREFERENCES: Rotting fruit, sap, flowers such as butterfly bush, milkweed, moss pink, New Jersey tea, rock cress, dogbane, mountain andromeda, pussy willows, composites such as Shasta daisy.

ON WING: Year-round.

BROODS: One-three.

HIBERNATES AS: Adult.

HABITATS: Open woodlands, riversides, forest edges.

SPECIAL FEATURES: Possibly the longest-lived North American butterfly, it may survive for more than ten months. Often the first butterfly on wing in spring, as it comes out of hibernation. Eggs laid in clusters. Caterpillars feed communally in a silk web at first, singly during the last two instars. Perches on branches, stumps, and other features (even an outstretched hand) for pursuit of mate. A fine garden butterfly that may surprise you by flying in February.

Painted Lady

(*Vanessa cardui*)

RANGE: Entire U.S., but ephemeral.

FOODPLANT: Various members of the daisy family (Compositae), including thistle (*Cirsium*), knapweed (*Centaurea*), burdock (*Arctium*), groundsel (*Senecio*), sunflower (*Helianthus*), pearly everlasting (*Anaphalis margaritacea*), wormwood (*Artemisia*); members of the borage family (*Boraginaceae*); members of the mallow family (Malvaceae), including hollyhock (*Althaea*), common mallow (*Malva neglecta*).

NECTAR PREFERENCES: Composites such as thistle, dandelion, Joe-Pye weed, ironweed, gayfeather, rabbitbrush, aster, Michaelmas daisy, zinnia, cosmos, and dahlia; also butterfly bush, buttonbush, bee balm, mint, sweet William, valerian, red clover, showy stonecrop, privet, candytuft, milkweed, Siberian wallflower, scabiosa, mallow.

ON WING: Spring-fall in North, year-round in far South.

BROODS: One-four.

HIBERNATES AS: Unable to overwinter in cold areas.

HABITATS: Open areas, meadows, mountains, deserts.

SPECIAL FEATURES: Mass emigrations repopulate North America from the South each year. Number of emigrants fluctuates from year to year, but occasionally reaches monumental proportions. Weak southward emigrations may occur in autumn. The "Cosmopolitan Butterfly" is a beloved garden visitor worldwide.

Pearl Crescent

(*Phyciodes tharos*)

RANGE: Entire U.S. except Pacific Coast.

FOODPLANT: Various species of aster (*Aster*).

NECTAR PREFERENCES: Composites such as aster, thistle, showy daisy, black-eyed Susan, hawkweed, fleabane, beggarticks, and tickseed sunflower; also dogbane, white clover, sticky geranium, winter cress, milkweed, peppermint.

ON WING: April-November, year-round in far South.

BROODS: One-five, or more.

HIBERNATES AS: Half-grown caterpillar.

HABITATS: Open areas, fields, moist meadows, streamsides, roadsides.

SPECIAL FEATURES: Pugnacious or inquisitive butterfly, often darting after passing objects. Newly emerged males visit moist ground and streamsides and patrol their territories in the garden. Eggs laid in clusters, larvae feed communally.

Queen

(Danaus gilippus)

RANGE: Entire southern U.S.; occasionally strays northward.

FOODPLANT: Various species of milkweed (*Asclepias*).

NECTAR PREFERENCES: Milkweed, fogfruit, (*Lippia lanceolata*), beggar-ticks, various daisies.

ON WING: April-November, year-round in far South.

BROODS: Multiple.

HIBERNATES AS: None, cannot overwinter in the North.

HABITATS: Open areas, meadows, fields, roadsides, prairies, deserts, waterways.

SPECIAL FEATURES: Distasteful to predators. Mimicked by the darker form of the Viceroy. Some individuals emigrate northward. Southern butterfly gardeners find this a very special resource. Males visit madder vine.

Question Mark

(Polygonia interrogationis)

RANGE: Entire U.S. east of Rockies.

FOODPLANT: Nettle (*Urtica*), false nettle (*Boehmeria cylindrica*), hops (*Humulus*), elm (*Ulmus*), hackberry (*Celtis*).

NECTAR PREFERENCES: Rotting fruit, sap, dung, carrion, flowers such as aster, milkweed, sweet pepperbush.

ON WING: Spring to fall.

BROODS: Two-five.

HIBERNATES AS: Adult.

HABITATS: Open woodlands, streamsides, orchards, roadsides.

SPECIAL FEATURES: Silvery "question mark" on underside of each hindwing, formed by a swirl and nearby dot. Butterfly emigrates widely in the fall, and sometimes overwinters in large groups. May become intoxicated by drinking the juices of fermented fruit. Males often land on tree trunks, visit mud, and exhibit territorial behavior. Females usually oviposit on a plant near the host, laying their eggs in columns, horizontal strings, or singly.

Red Admiral

(*Vanessa atalanta*)

RANGE: Entire U.S. during summer and fall.

FOODPLANT: Various members of the nettle family (Urticaceae), including stinging nettle (*Urtica dioica*), tall wild nettle (*U. gracilis*), false nettle (*Boehmeria cylindrica*), wood nettle (*Laportea canadensis*), pellitory (*Parietaria*), hops (*Humulus*).

NECTAR PREFERENCES: Rotting fruit, sap, composites such as Michaelmas daisy, aster, thistle, dandelion, gumweed, daisy, goldenrod, beggar-ticks, Gloriosa daisy, Shasta daisy, gayfeather, dahlia, and ageratum; also butterfly bush, milkweed, candytuft, alfalfa, showy stonecrop, dogbane, Siberian wallflower, hebe, sweet pepperbush, ivy, fireweed, red clover, mallow, sea holly, mint, valerian.

ON WING: April-October, year-round in the far South.

BROODS: One-three.

HIBERNATES AS: Rarely as an adult; generally unable to over-winter in North.

HABITATS: Open woodlands, forest edges, meadows, stream-sides, roadsides, yards, and parks.

SPECIAL FEATURES: Emigrates north each spring. Some individuals may emigrate south in autumn. Acts territorial, male perches and darts out after females and other passing objects, often alights on people in gardens, and is generally well habit-uated to human environments. Caterpillars make nettle-leaf shelters and help keep nettles in check. A favorite of many gardeners.

Red-spotted Admiral

(*Limenitis arthemis astyanax*)

RANGE: Entire U.S. east of Rockies; southern Arizona.

FOODPLANT: Willow (*Salix*), aspen, poplar (*Populus*), cherry, plum (*Prunus*), oak (*Quercus*), hawthorn (*Crataegus*), apple (*Malus*), hornbeam (*Carpinus*), gooseberry (*Ribes*), deerberry (*Vaccinium stamineum*).

NECTAR PREFERENCES: Rotting fruit, sap, dung, carrion, aphid honeydew, flowers such as cardinal flower, viburnum, spi-raea, privet, Hercules-club, sweet pepperbush.

ON WING: May–October, earlier in far South.

BROODS: Two-three.

HIBERNATES AS: Young caterpillar.

HABITATS: Open woodlands, forest edges, streamsides, meadows.

SPECIAL FEATURES: Mimics the Pipevine Swallowtail. Often basks on roads and sidewalks, displaying its brilliant metallic-blue wings.

Satyr Comma

(*Polygonia satyrus*)

RANGE: Western U.S. from eastern edge of Rockies to the Pacific; occasionally in extreme north of eastern U.S.

FOODPLANT: Nettle (*Urtica*).

NECTAR PREFERENCES: Rotting fruit, sap, flowers such as blackberry, almond.

ON WING: Early spring to late fall.

BROODS: Two or more.

HIBERNATES AS: Adult.

HABITATS: Open woodlands, streamsides, roadsides, parks, and glades.

SPECIAL FEATURES: Fond of dappled riverbanks. Camouflaged against tree bark, startles birds with bright upperside revealed in flight. Likes to bask in bright sun with wings spread open.

Viceroy

(*Limenitis archippus*)

RANGE: Most of U.S. from Atlantic west through Great Basin.

FOODPLANT: Willow (*Salix*), aspen, poplar (*Populus*), apple (*Malus*), plum, cherry (*Prunus*).

NECTAR PREFERENCES: Rotting fruit, sap, dung, carrion, aphid honeydew, composites such as thistle, aster, Joe-Pye weed, goldenrod, and beggar-ticks; also milkweed.

ON WING: April–September, almost year-round farther South.

BROODS: One or two in North, three or more in South.

HIBERNATES AS: Young caterpillar.

HABITATS: Open areas, streamsides, marshes, meadows, roadsides.

SPECIAL FEATURES: Palatable mimic of the distasteful Monarch. In the southern part of range, mimics the darker Queen. Behavior and biology similar to White Admiral and Red-spotted Admiral, since they are all closely related admirals despite their different appearances.

West Coast Lady

(*Vanessa annabella*)

RANGE: Western U.S. from Great Plains to Pacific Coast.

FOODPLANT: Various members of the mallow family (Malvaceae), including cheeseweed (*Malva parviflora*), hollyhock (*Althaea*), globemallow (*Sphaeralcea*), sidalcea (*Sidalcea*); nettle (*Urtica*).

NECTAR PREFERENCES: Butterfly bush, cheeseweed, mallow, mint, statice, composites such as aster, thistle, marigold.

ON WING: Early spring to late fall, year-round in far South.

BROODS: Multiple.

HIBERNATES AS: May not be able to resist frost in any stage.

HABITATS: Open areas, fields, mountains.

SPECIAL FEATURES: Population fluctuates from year to year, but without the Painted Lady's mass movement. Some individuals emigrate, for example, into the Rockies from farther west. Butterfly fond of basking on bare ground and hilltops with other individuals.

White Admiral

(*Limenitis arthemis arthemis*)

RANGE: Northeastern U.S. from Minnesota to New England.

FOODPLANT: Birch (*Betula*), aspen, poplar (*Populus*), willow (*Salix*), hawthorn (*Crataegus*), basswood (*Tilia*), American hornbeam (*Carpinus caroliniana*), shadbush (Amelanchier).

NECTAR PREFERENCES: Rotting fruit, sap, dung, carrion, aphid honeydew, various flowers.

ON WING: June–August.

BROODS: One–two.

HIBERNATES AS: Young caterpillar.

HABITATS: Open woodlands, forest edges, roadsides.

SPECIAL FEATURES: Often perches high above ground, then darts out after passing objects. Caterpillar overwinters in a hibernaculum constructed from a rolled-up leaf. These may be found and brought into the garden for emergence in spring.

SKIPPERS

(*Hesperiidae*)

Common Checkered-Skipper

(*Pyrgus communis*)

RANGE: Entire U.S. except northern New England and coastal Northwest.

FOODPLANT: Various members of the mallow family (Malvaceae), including mallow (*Malva*), cheeseweed (*Malva parviflora*), hollyhock (*Althaea*), hibiscus (*Hibiscus*), *Sida*, *Sidalcea*, velvet-leaf (*Abutilon*), globe mallow (*Sphaeralcea*), poppy mallow (*Callirhoe*).

NECTAR PREFERENCES: Composites such as aster, knapweed, red clover, fleabane, mistflower, and beggar-ticks; red clover.

ON WING: March–October, year-round in far South.

BROODS: Three or more.

HIBERNATES AS: Chrysalis or full-grown caterpillar.

HABITATS: Open woodlands, meadows, prairies, roadsides, riversides, vacant lots.

SPECIAL FEATURES: Emigrates widely, but also forms small colonies readily. Scarcely a vacant lot in its range lacks this butterfly patrolling back and forth. Its grayish colors and whirring flight make it appear bluish on the wing.

Fiery Skipper

(*Hylephila phyleus*)

RANGE: Eastern and southwestern U.S.

FOODPLANT: Various species of grasses (Poaceae), including Bermuda grass (*Cynodon dactylon*), St. Augustine grass (*Stenotaphrum secundatum*), bent grass (*Agrostis*), crabgrass (*Digitaria*), sugar cane (*Saccharum officinarum*).

NECTAR PREFERENCES: Lantana, aster, milkweed, thistle, glossy abelia, sweet pepperbush, statice, Cape plumbago, sneezeweed, beggar-ticks, Felicia daisy, ironweed, bristly ox tongue, knapweed.

ON WING: Year-round in far South, shorter period farther north.

BROODS: Two-five.

HIBERNATES AS: Unable to overwinter in North.

HABITATS: Lawns, grasslands, fields, forest edges, roadsides.

SPECIAL FEATURES: Emigrates northward in spring. Audible when fluttering wings. Males perch and dart out after females and other passing objects. Caterpillars construct shelters at base of grass and thereby escape damage from lawn mowers. A delightful and bright city skipper throughout its regular range.

Silver-spotted Skipper

(*Epargyreus clarus*)

RANGE: Entire U.S., but sporadic.

FOODPLANT: Various members of the pea family (Leguminosae), including locust (*Robinia, Gleditsia*), wisteria (*Wisteria*), tick-trefoil (*Desmodium*), hog peanut (*Amphicarpa bracteata*), beans (*Phaseolus*), kudzu (*Peuraria thunbergii*), acacia (*Acacia*), licorice (*Glycyrrhiza*).

NECTAR PREFERENCES: Honeysuckle, thistle, Joe-Pye weed, gayfeather, zinnia, milkweed, iris, buttonbush, dogbane, viper's bugloss, everlasting pea, privet, winter cress, red clover, purple vetch, self-heal.

ON WING: May-September, year-round in far South.

BROODS: One in far North, two-four in South.

HIBERNATES AS: Caterpillar, in leaf tent.

HABITATS: Open woodlands, hillsides, roadsides, suburbs.

SPECIAL FEATURES: Exhibits territorial and seemingly pugnacious behavior, as males perch and occasionally patrol, searching for females. Audible when fluttering wings. Caterpillars construct shelters from leaves of the foodplant and overwinter in them, then pupate in a loose cocoon among debris on the ground. A big, flashy skipper as happy in gardens as in wild habitats.

Tawny-edged Skipper

(*Polites themistocles*)

RANGE: Entire U.S., except most of Northwest.

FOODPLANT: Various species of grasses (Poaceae), including panic grass (*Panicum*), and bluegrass (*Poa*).

NECTAR PREFERENCES: Thistle, red clover, chicory, alfalfa, purple coneflower, *Houstonia,* dogbane.

ON WING: April-September, year-round in Florida.

BROODS: One-two or more.

HIBERNATES AS: Chrysalis.

HABITATS: Grasslands, open woodlands, moist meadows, fields, roadsides, lawns.

SPECIAL FEATURES: Prefers grasslands in East, open forest and boggy mountain lakesides in West. In the Midwest, it is the most common skipper of lawns. Not a pest, its ability to colonize lawn grass makes it an ideal garden butterfly.

Nectar Sources

Cultivated Plants

abelia (*Abelia*) shrub; white, pink, purple; summer–early fall

ageratum (*Ageratum*) annual; blue, white, pink; summer–fall

alder buckthorn (*Rhamnus frangula*) shrub or small tree; white; spring–summer

allium (*Allium*) bulb; pink, rose, violet, red, blue, yellow, white; late spring–summer

alyssum (*Alyssum*) perennial; yellow, white, pink; spring–fall

alyssum, sweet (*Lobularia maritima*) annual; white, pink, violet; spring–summer, longer in warmer areas

anemone (*Anemone*) perennial; blue, red, white, pink, rose, purple; early spring–fall

anthemis (*Anthemis*) perennial; yellow; summer–fall

arabis (*Arabis*) perennial; white, pink, purple; spring

aralia (*Aralia*) shrub-tree; white; midsummer

aster (*Aster*) perennial; white, blue, red, purple; spring–fall

astilbe (*Astilbe*) perennial; white, pink, red; May–July

aubrieta, common (*Aubrieta deltoidea*) perennial; red, purple; early spring

barberry (*Berberis*) shrub; yellow, white; spring

beauty bush (*Kolkwitzia amabilis*) shrub; pink; May–June

bellflower (*Campanula*) perennial, biennial, annual; blue, purple, lavender, violet, white; spring–fall

blackberry; bramble (*Rubus*) shrub; white, pink; summer–fall

blackthorn (*Prunus spinosa*) shrub; white; spring

bleeding heart (*Dicentra*) perennial; pink, rose, white, yellow; spring–fall

blueberry; huckleberry (*Vaccinium*) shrub; white, pink; spring

buckeye (*Aesculus*) tree or large shrub; creamy; spring

buddleia (*Buddleia*) shrub or small tree; white, pink, violet; midsummer–fall

butterfly bush (*Buddleia davidii*) shrub or small tree; lilac with orange eye; midsummer–fall

butterfly weed (*Asclepias tuberosa*) perennial; orange; midsummer–early fall

buttonbush (*Cephalanthus occidentalis*) shrub or small tree; white; summer

calendula (*Calendula officinalis*) annual; orange, yellow; spring–midsummer; late fall through spring in milder areas

candytuft (*Iberis*) annual, perennial; white, pink, rose, purple, lavender, red; early spring–summer

Cape plumbago (*Plumbago auriculata*) shrub; blue, white; spring–fall, longer in warmer areas

caryopteris (*Caryopteris*) shrub; blue; late summer–fall

catmint (*Nepeta mussinii*) perennial; blue; early summer

catnip (*Nepeta cataria*) perennial; lavender, white; early summer

ceanothus (*Ceanothus*) shrub, small tree, ground cover; white, blue, pink; spring

cherry (*Prunus*) tree; white, pink; spring–fall

chestnut (*Castanea*) tree; white; summer

chives (*Allium schoenoprasum*) perennial; purple; spring

cinquefoil (*Potentilla*) perennial, shrub; yellow, white, pink; spring–fall

clematis (*Clematis*) vine, perennial; white, red, violet, pink, blue; spring–fall

coneflower, purple (*Echinacea purpurea*) perennial; purple; late summer

coreopsis (*Coreopsis*) annual, perennial; yellow, orange, red; late spring–fall

cornflower (*Centaurea cyanus*) annual; blue, pink, rose, red, white; summer

cosmos (*Cosmos*) annual; white, pink, rose, purple, yellow, lavender; summer–fall

cotoneaster (*Cotoneaster*) shrub; white, pink; spring

daffodil (*Narcissus*) bulb; yellow and white, with variations of orange, red, pink; spring

dahlia (*Dahlia*) perennial; many colors; summer–fall

daisy (*Chrysanthemum*) and other genera (see below)

daisy, gloriosa (*Rudbeckia hirta*) biennial or short-lived perennial, can be grown as an annual; yellow, orange, russet; summer–fall

daisy, Michaelmas (*Aster novi-belgii*) perennial; white, pink, rose, red, blue, violet, purple; late summer daisy, Shasta (*Chrysanthemum maximum*) perennial; white, yellow; summer–fall

daisy bush (*Olearia haastii*) shrub; white; summer

daylily (*Hemerocallis*) perennial; orange, red, yellow, white; spring–fall

deutzia (*Deutzia*) shrub; white, pink; May–June

echium (*Echium*) biennial or shrubby perennial; blue, purple, rose, red; mid to late spring

English laurel (*Prunus laurocerasus*) shrub or small tree; white; summer

escallonia (*Escallonia*) shrub; red, white, pink; summer–fall, nearly year-round in mild climates

fleabane (*Erigeron*) perennial; white, pink, lavender, violet; early summer–fall

flowering tobacco (*Nicotiana*) perennial; white, red; summer

forget-me-not (*Myosotis*) annual, biennial, perennial; blue; early spring–fall

gaillardia (*Gaillardia*) perennial, annual; yellow, red, white, bronze; summer–fall

gayfeather (*Liatris*) perennial; purple; summer

gazania (*Gazania*) perennial; yellow, orange, white, pink; late spring and early summer, intermittently throughout the year in mild areas

geranium (*Pelargonium*) perennial; white, pink, red, purple, rose, lavender, violet, orange; summer, longer where protected

globe thistle (*Echinops exaltatus*) perennial; blue; midsummer–late fall

goldenrod (*Solidago*) perennial; yellow; summer–fall

gooseberry (*Ribes*) shrub; yellow, pink, red, purple; spring

hawkweed (*Hieracium*) biennial; yellow; midsummer

hawthorn (*Crataegus*) shrub or tree; white; spring

hazel (*Corylus avellana*) shrub; yellow; early spring

heath (*Erica*) shrub; white, red, pink, purple; year-round, depending on species.

heather (*Calluna*) shrub; pink, white, purple, lavender; summer–fall

hebe (*Hebe*) shrub; white, blue, purple, red; late spring–fall

heliotrope (*Heliotropium*) perennial; violet, white; spring–summer

honesty (*Lunaria annua*) biennial; purple, pink, white; late spring–early summer

honeysuckle (*Lonicera*) shrub or vine; orange, white, pink, red, purple, rose; early spring–fall hyssop (*Hyssopus officinalis*) perennial; blue, white, pink, purple; midsummer–late fall

impatiens (*Impatiens*) annual, perennial; white, pink, rose, purple, red, orange, lavender; summer

ivy, English (*Hedera helix*) vine; greenish; late fall–winter

Jacob's ladder (*Polemonium caeruleum*) perennial; blue; spring–summer

Jupiter's beard (*Centranthus ruber*) perennial; red, white; late spring–early summer

lantana (*Lantana*) shrub; yellow, orange, red, purple, white, pink, lavender; year-round in frost-free areas

lavender (*Lavandula*) shrub; lavender, purple; almost year-round in mild areas

lilac (*Syringa*) shrub; purple, white, pink, lavender; spring

lily (*Lilium*) bulb; many colors; generally late summer

lily of the Nile (*Agapanthus*) perennial; blue, white, purple; midsummer–early fall

linanthus (*Linanthus*) annual; lavender, white, pink, yellow; spring

lippia (*Phyla nodiflora*) perennial; purple, rose; spring–fall

lobelia (*Lobelia*) perennial, annual; red, blue, pink, purple, violet, white; early summer–late fall; winter in mild areas

lupine (*Lupinus*) annual, perennial, shrub; yellow, blue, white, pink, purple, red, orange; early spring–fall

marigold (*Tagetes*) annual; yellow, orange, maroon; early summer–late fall if old flowers are picked off

marjoram (*Origanum vulgare*) perennial; pink; midsummer

meadow saffron (*Colchicum autumnale*) corm; pink, purple, white; late summer

Mexican orange (*Choisyaternata*) shrub; white; early spring–summer

mignonette (*Reseda odorata*) annual; greenish-yellow; early spring–summer

mint (*Mentha*) perennial; purple; summer

mock orange (*Philadelphus*) shrub; white; late spring–early summer

monkshood (*Aconitum*) perennial; blue, purple; fall

nasturtium (*Tropaeolum*) perennial, generally grown as an annual; red, orange, yellow, white, bicolored; late summer

passion flower (*Passiflora*) vine; white, purple, pink, blue; summer pear (*Pyrus communis*) tree; white; early spring

petunia (*Petunia*) tender perennial, grown as an annual; pink, red, blue, purple, white; summer

phlox (*Phlox*) annual, perennial; white, purple, blue, pink, red, rose, lavender; spring–summer

pink (*Dianthus*) perennial, biennial, annual; pink, rose, red, yellow, orange; spring or summer, sometimes until frost

plum (*Prunus*) tree; white, pink; early spring

polyanthus (*Primula polyantha*) perennial; many colors; winter–spring

primrose (*Primula*) perennial; many colors; early spring–summer, sometimes longer

privet (*Ligustrum*) shrub or small tree; white; late spring–early summer

purple loosestrife (*Lythrum salicaria*) perennial; magenta, late summer

pussy willow (*Salix discolor*) shrub or small tree; pearl gray becoming yellow; late winter or early spring

redbud (*Cercis*) shrub or tree; pink, white, red, rose, purple; early spring

red-hot poker (*Kniphofia uvaria*) perennial; red, yellow, white; spring–summer

rockrose (*Cistus*) shrub; pink, white, purple; late spring–summer.

rosemary (*Rosmarinus officinalis*) shrub; blue, purple; spring–fall

rose of Sharon (*Hibiscus syriacus*) shrub; white, red, blue, pink, purple; summer

sage (*Salvia*) annual, perennial, shrub; blue, purple, red, white, rose, lavender; late spring–late fall

scabiosa (*Scabiosa*) annual, perennial; purple, pink, blue, white, rose; June–late fall

sea holly (*Eryngium amethystinum*) perennial; blue, purple; midsummer–fall

senecio (*Senecio*) perennial, shrub, vine; yellow, red, white, pink, blue, purple; year-round in mild areas

showy stonecrop (*Sedum spectabile*) perennial; pink, rose, red; late summer–fall

snapdragon (*Antirrhinum*) perennial, usually treated as an annual; many colors; spring–summer sneezeweed, common (*Helenium autumnale*) perennial; yellow, orange, red; summer–fall

spiraea (*Spiraea*) shrub; white, pink, red; spring–fall

spurge (*Euphorbia*) shrub, perennial, biennial, annual; yellow, orange, pink; late winter–spring

St. Johnswort (*Hypericum*) shrub, perennial; yellow; summer

star clusters *(Pentas lanceolata)* perennial, usually treated as annual; white, red, purple, pink; various times throughout year.

statice (*Limonium*) annual, perennial; yellow, blue, purple, pink, white; spring–summer

stonecrop (*Sedum*) perennial; yellow, white, pink, red; spring–fall

sumac (*Rhus*) shrub or tree; white, pink, greenish; almost year-round in warm areas

sunflower (*Helianthus*) annual, perennial; yellow, orange, red-brown; late summer–fall

sunrose (*Helianthemum nummularium*) shrub; red, orange, yellow, pink, rose, white; spring–summer

sweet rocket (*Hesperis matronalis*) perennial; purple, white; spring–summer

sweet William (*Dianthus barbatus*) biennial, often grown as an annual; white, pink, rose, red, purple, bicolored; spring–summer

thrift (*Armeria*) perennial; white, pink, rose, red; early spring–late fall

thyme (*Thymus*) perennial; pink, white, purple; June–September

tidytips (*Layia platyglossa*) annual; yellow; summer

toadflax (*Linaria*) annual, perennial; many colors, June–September

valerian (*Valeriana officinalis*) perennial; white, pink, blue; mid–late summer

verbena (*Verbena*) perennial, some grown as annuals; white, pink, red, purple, blue; summer

viburnum (*Viburnum*) shrubs, rarely small trees; white, pink; early spring–summer

violet (*Viola*) perennial, some treated as annuals; white, blue, purple; spring–summer

viper's bugloss (*Echium vulgare*) annual; blue, purple, rose, white lavender; late summer

vitex (*Vitex*) shrub or tree; blue, white, pink; summer–fall wallflower (*Cheiranthus cheiri*) perennial, biennial; yellow, orange, brown, red, pink, burgundy; spring–early summer

weigela (*Weigela*) shrub; red, white, pink, yellow; spring–fall

yarrow (*Achillea*) perennial; white, yellow, red; summer–early fall

zinnia (*Zinnia*) annual; many colors; summer–early fall

Native Plants

alfalfa (*Medicago sativa*) blue, purple; May–October, year–round in some areas; widespread across U.S.

alpine sunflower (*Hymenoxys grandiflora*) yellow; July–October; western U.S.

aster (*Aster*) pink, purple, blue, white; June–November; widespread across U.S.

aster, New England (*Aster novae-angliae*) purple, rose; August–October; eastern U.S.

beggar-ticks; bur-marigold (*Bidens*) yellow; July–November; widespread across U.S.

bindweed, field (*Convolvulus arvensis*) white, pink; April–October; widespread across U.S.

blackberry; bramble (*Rubus*) white; May–July; widespread across U.S.

blackberry-lily (*Belamcanda chinensis*) orange; June–July; eastern U.S.

black-eyed Susan (*Rudbeckia hirta*) yellow; June–October; eastern U.S. and Rockies

blazing star (*Liatris*) purple; July to frost; eastern U.S. and Rockies

bluebell (*Campanulaceae*) blue; May–August; widespread across U.S.

boneset (*Eupatorium perfoliatum*) white, purple; July–October; eastern U.S.

bouncing bet (*Saponana officinalis*) pink, white; July–September; eastern U.S.

bugle (*Ajuga reptans*) blue; May–July; eastern U.S.

buttercup (*Ranunculus*) yellow; February–September; widespread across U.S.

butterfly weed (*Asclepias tuberosa*) orange, red; June–September; eastern U.S.

campion (*Silene*) white, pink; April–October; widespread across U.S.

campion, red (*Lychnis dioica*) red; June–September; northern part of eastern U.S.

cat's-ear (*Hypochoeris radicata*) yellow; March–August; northern part of eastern U.S., West

cinquefoil (*Potentilla*) yellow, purple, white, red; March–October; widespread across U.S.

clover, red (*Trifolium pratense*) red; April–October; widespread across U.S.

clover, white (*Trifolium repens*) white; May–October, year-round in some areas; widespread across U.S.

coltsfoot (*Tussilago farfara*) yellow; March–June; eastern U.S.

comfrey (*Symphytum officinale*) white, pink, purple, blue, yellow; June–September; eastern U.S.

coneflower (*Echinacea, Rudbeckia*) yellow; July–October; widespread across U. S.

cornflower (*Centaurea cyanus*) blue, pink, white, purple; May–October; East, West

cuckoo-flower (*Cardamine pratensis*) white, pink; April–June; eastern U.S.

daisy, ox-eye (*Chrysanthemum leucanthemum*) white; May–October; East, West

dame's rocket (*Hesperis matronalis*) pink, purple, white; May–July; eastern U.S.

dandelion (*Taraxacum officinale*) yellow; early spring–late fall, year-round in some areas; widespread across U.S.

daylily (*Hemerocallis fulva*) orange; June–August; eastern U.S.

field scabious (*Knautia arvensis*) lavender; June–August; eastern U.S.

field sow–thistle (*Sonchus arvensis*) yellow; July–October; eastern U.S. and Rockies

figwort (*Scrophularia lanceolata*) green and brown; May–July; eastern U.S.

fireweed (*Epilobium angustifolium*) pink, purple; June–September; widespread across U.S.

flame azalea (*Rhododendron calendulaceum*) orange; May–June; eastern U.S.

fleabane, common (*Erigeron philadelphicus*) pink, purple, white; March–July; East, West

goatsbeard (*Tragopogon pratensis*) yellow; June–October; widespread across U.S.

golden Alexanders (*Zizia aurea*) yellow; April–June; eastern U.S.

goldenrod (*Solidago*) yellow; May–November; widespread across U.S.

groundsel, common (*Senecio vulgaris*) yellow; May–October, year-round in some areas; widespread across U.S.

harebell (*Campanula rotundifolia*) blue; June–September; widespread across U.S.

hawkweed (*Hieracium*) yellow, orange, white; May–October; widespread across U.S.

hawthorn (*Crataegus*) white, pink, red; May–June; widespread across U.S.

heather (*Calluna vulgaris*) pink; July–November; eastern U.S.

honeysuckle (*Lonicera*) yellow, white, orange; April–September; eastern U.S., Rockies, Northwest

hound's-tongue (*Cynoglossum officinale*) purple; May–August; widespread across U.S.

Indian hemp (*Apocynum cannabinum*) white, pink; June–September; East, West

ironweed (*Vernonia*) purple; July–October; eastern U.S.

Joe-Pye weed (*Eupatorium*) purple; July–September; eastern U.S.

knapweed (*Centaurea*) pink, purple, white, rose; May–October; widespread across U.S.

lesser celandine (*Ranunculus ficaria*) yellow; April–June; eastern U.S.

lupine (*Lupinus*) blue, purple, pink, white, yellow; December–October; widespread across U.S.

mallow (*Malva*) pink, white, lavender; April–October, year-round in some areas; East, West

meadowsweet (*Spiraea latifolia*) pink, white; June–September; eastern U.S.

milkweed (*Asclepias*) many colors; April–August, March–December in some areas; widespread across U.S.

mustard (*Brassica*) yellow, white; January–October; East, West

New Jersey tea (*Ceanothus americanus*) shrub; white; spring–summer

phlox (*Phlox*) many colors; April–October; widespread across U.S.

primrose (*Primula*) pink, white, red, purple, blue; March–August; widespread across U.S.

purple loosestrife (*Lythrum salicaria*) purple; June–September; East, West

Queen Anne's lace (*Daucus carota*) white; May–October, year-round in
    some areas; East, West
ragged-robin (*Lychnis flos-cuculi*) pink, white; June–July; eastern U.S.
ragwort (*Senecio*) yellow; April–August; widespread across U.S.
sage (*Salvia*) blue, white, yellow, purple; March–July; East, West
self-heal (*Prunella vulgaris*) purple, blue; May–September; East, West
spearmint (*Mentha spicata*) purple, pink; June–October; widespread across
    U.S.
sunflower (*Helianthus*) yellow; June–October, February–November in
    some areas; widespread across U.S.
sweet-William catchfly (*Silene armeria*) pink; June–October; eastern U.S.
thistle (*Cirsium*) purple, white, yellow, rose, red; April–October; wide-
    spread across U.S.
toadflax (*Linaria vulgaris*) yellow; June–October; eastern U.S.
valerian (*Valeriana officinalis*) pink; June–July; eastern U.S.
verbena, vervain (*Verbena*) blue, purple, pink, white; June–September;
    East, West
violet (*Viola*) violet, white, blue, yellow; December–August; widespread
    across U.S.
water mint (*Mentha aquatica*) lavender; August–October; eastern U.S.
wild bergamot (*Monarda fistulosa*) purple; July–August; eastern U.S.
wild cherry (*Prunus*) white; April–May; widespread across U.S.
wild gooseberry (*Ribes*) yellow, white, pink; late April–early June; wide-
    spread across U.S.
wild lilac (*Ceanothus sanguineus*) blue; June–July; western U.S.
wild parsnip (*Pastinaca sativa*) yellow; May–October; eastern U.S.
woundwort (*Stachys palustris*) magenta; July–September; eastern U.S.
yarrow (*Achillea millefolium*) white, pink; March–November; widespread
    across U.S.
yellow bedstraw (*Galium verum*) yellow; June–August; northern part of
    eastern U.S.
yellow vetchling (*Lathyrus pratensis*) yellow; June–August; eastern U.S.

Bibliography

Butterflies

Allen, James. "How to Photograph Butterflies." *Terra* 23/5 (1985):25–30.

Allen, Thomas J.; Brock, Jim P.; and Glassberg, Jeffrey. *Caterpillars in the Field and Garden: A Field Guide to the Butterfly Caterpillars of North America.* New York: Oxford University Press, 2005.

Arnett, Dr. Ross H. Jr., and Jacques, Dr. Richard L., Jr. *Simon and Schuster's Guide to Insects.* New York: Simon and Schuster, 1981.

Bernard, Gary D. "Red-absorbing Visual Pigment of Butterflies." *Science* 203 (1979):1125–27.

Borror, Donald J., and White, Richard E. *A Field Guide to the Insects of America North of Mexico.* Boston: Houghton Mifflin, 1970.

Brewer, Jo. *Wings in the Meadow.* New York: Houghton Mifflin, 1967.

Brock, Jim P., and Kaufman, Kenn. *Field Guide to Butterflies of North America.* Boston: Houghton Mifflin, 2003.

Brower, Lincoln P. "Ecological Chemistry." *Scientific American* 220/2 (1969):22–29.

Brower, Lincoln P. "Monarch Migration." *Natural History,* June/July, 1977.

Brown, F. Martin. *Colorado Butterflies.* Denver: Denver Museum of Natural History, 1957.

Christensen, James R. *A Field Guide to the Butterflies of the Pacific Northwest.* Moscow, Idaho: The University Press of Idaho, 1981.

Comstock, John Adams. *Butterflies of California.* Los Angeles: published by the author, 1927.

Comstock, John Henry, and Comstock, Anna Botsford. *How to Know the Butterflies.* New York: D. Appleton and Company, 1904.

Dethier, V.G., and MacArthur, Robert H. "A Field's Capacity to Support a Butterfly Population." *Nature* 201 (1964):728–29.

Donahue, Julian P. "Strategies For Survival: the Cause of a Caterpillar." *Terra* 17/4 (1979):3–9.

Dornfeld, Ernst J. *The Butterflies of Oregon.* Beaverton, OR: Timber Press, 1980.

Dronamraju, K.R. "Selective Visits of Butterflies to Flowers: A Possible Factor in Sympatric Speciation." *Nature* 186 (1960):178.

Ebner, James A. *The Butterflies of Wisconsin.* Milwaukee Public Museum: *Popular Science Handbook,* 1970.

Ehrlich, Paul R., and Ehrlich, Anne H. *How to Know the Butterflies.* Dubuque: Wm. C. Brown, 1961.

Ehrlich, Paul R., and Raven, Peter H. "Butterflies and Plants." *Scientific American* 216/6 (1967):104–13.

Eisner, T.; Silberglied, R.E.; Aneshansley, D.; Carrel, J.E.; and Howland, H.C. "Ultraviolet Video-Viewing: the Television Camera as an Insect Eye." *Science* 166 (1969): 1172–74.

Emmel, Thomas C. *Butterflies: Their World, Their Life Cycle, Their Behavior.* New York: Alfred A. Knopf, 1975.

Emmel, Thomas C., and Emmel, John F. *The Butterflies of Southern California.* Los Angeles: Natural History Museum of Los Angeles County, 1973.

Ferguson, D.C. *Host Records for Lepidoptera Reared in Eastern North America.* Washington, D.C.: Agricultural Research Service, United States Department of Agriculture, Technical Bulletin No. 1521 (1975).

Ferris, Clifford D., and Brown, Martin F., eds. *Butterflies of the Rocky Mountain States.* Norman: University of Oklahoma Press, 1981.

Field, William D. *A Manual of the Butterflies and Skippers of Kansas.* Bulletin of the University of Kansas 39/10 (1938):3–328.

Ford, E. B. *Butterflies.* Revised edition. Glasgow: Collins, 1975.

Free, J.B.; Gennard, Dorothy; Stevenson, J.H.; and Williams, Ingrid H. "Beneficial Insects Present on a Motorway Verge." *Biological Conservation* 8 (1975):61–72.

Garth, John S., and Tilden, J.W. "Yosemite Butterflies: An Ecological Survey of the Butterflies of the Yosemite Sector of the Sierra Nevada, California." *The Journal of Research on the Lepidoptera* 2/1 (1963): 1–96.

Gilbert, Lawrence E. "Ecological Consequences of a Coevolved Mutualism Between Butterflies and Plants." In *Coevolution of Animals and Plants.* Austin: University of Texas Press, 1975.

Gilbert, Lawrence E., and Singer, Michael C. "Butterfly Ecology." *Annual Review of Ecology and Systematics* 6 (1975):365–97.

Glassberg, Jeffrey. *A Swift Guide to Butterflies of North America.* Morristown, NJ: Sunstreak Books, 2012.

———. *Butterflies of North America.* New York: Sterling, 2011.

———. *Butterflies through Binoculars: A Field Guide to the Butterflies of Eastern North America.* New York: Oxford University Press, 1999.

———. *Butterflies through Binoculars: A Field Guide to the Butterflies of Western North America.* New York: Oxford University Press, 2001.

Hamm, A.H. "Butterflies at Oxford." *The Entomologist's Monthly Magazine,* December, 1943: 279.

Hamm, A.H. "Butterflies and Silver-Y Moth (*Plusia gamma* L.) at Oxford." *The Entomologist's Monthly Magazine,* March, 1945: 58.

Hamm, A.H. "Butterfly and Other Visitors to Michaelmas Daisies." *The Entomologist's Monthly Magazine,* April, 1948: 91–93.

Hanson, F.E. "Comparative Studies on Induction of Food Choice Preferences in Lepidopterous Larvae." In *The Host-Plant in Relation to Insect Behavior and Reproduction.* New York: Plenum Press, 1976.

Harris, Lucien, Jr. *Butterflies of Georgia.* Norman: University of Oklahoma Press, 1972.

Headstrom, Richard. *Adventures with Insects.* New York: Dover Publications, 1982.

Heath, Fred. *An Introduction to Southern California Butterflies.* Missoula: Mountain Press Publishing, 2004.

Hogue, Charles L. "Butterfly Wings: Living Pointillism." Los Angeles County Museum of Natural History *Quarterly,* 6/4 (1968):4–11.

Holland, W.J. *The Butterfly Book.* Garden City, NY: Doubleday, Doran & Company, 1931.

Howe, Robert W. "Wings Over the Prairie." *Iowa Conservationist,* September, 1984.

Howe, William H. *Our Butterflies and Moths.* North Kansas City: True Color Publishing Company, 1963.

Howe, William H., ed. *The Butterflies of North America.* New York: Doubleday & Company, 1975.

Ilse, Dora. "New Observations on Responses to Colours in Egg-laying Butterflies." *Nature* 140 (1937):544–45.

Ilse, Dora, and Vaidya, Vidyadhar G. "Spontaneous Feeding Response to Colors in *Papilio demoleus* L." *Proceedings of the Indian Academy of Sciences* 43 (1956):23–31.

Kennedy. J.S. "Mechanisms of Host Plant Selection." In *Readings in Entomology.* Philadelphia: W.B. Saunders Company, 1972.

Klots, Alexander B. *A Field Guide to the Butterflies of North America, East of the Great Plains.* Boston: Houghton Mifflin, 1951.

Klots, Alexander B. "Flight of the Butterfly." *USAir,* June, 1983.

Klots, Alexander B., and Klots, Elsie B. *1001 Answers to Questions About Insects.* New York: Grosset & Dunlap, 1961.

Langer, H., and Struwe, G. "Spectral Absorption by Screening Pigment Granules in the Compound Eye of Butterflies (*Heliconius*)." *Journal of Comparative Physiology* 79 (1972):203–12.

Lovell, John H. "Butterfly-Flowers." In *The Flower and the Bee: Plant Life and Pollination.* New York: Charles Scribner's Sons, 1918.

Masters, John H. "Collecting Ithomiidae With Heliotrope." *Journal of the Lepidopterists' Society* 22 (1968): 108–10.

Miller, Lee D., and Brown, F. Martin. *A Catalogue/Checklist of the Butterflies of America North of Mexico.* The Lepidopterists' Society, Memoir No. 2, 1981.

Milne, Louis, and Margery. *The Audubon Society Field Guide to North American Insects and Spiders.* New York: Alfred A. Knopf, 1980.

Mitchell, Robert T., and Zim, Herbert S. *Butterflies and Moths.* New York: Golden Press, 1964.

Nabokov, Vladimir. "Butterflies." In *Speak, Memory: An Autobiography Revisited.* New York: G.P. Putnam's Sons, 1966.

Opler, Paul A. "Management of Prairie Habitats For Insect Conservation." *Journal of the Natural Areas Association* 1/4 (1981):3–6.

Opler, Paul A., and Krizek, George O. *Butterflies East of the Great Plains.* Baltimore: The John Hopkins University Press, 1984.

Ordish, George. *The Year of the Butterfly.* New York: Charles Scribner's Sons, 1975.

Orsak, Larry J. *The Butterflies of Orange County, California.* Irvine, CA: University of California, 1977.

Orsak, Larry J. "Buckwheat and the Bright Blue Copper." *Garden,* January/February, 1980.

Owen, Denis F. "Lessons From a Caterpillar Plague in London's Berkeley Square." *Environmental Conservation,* 2/3 (1975):171–77.

Parenti, Umberto. *The World of Butterflies and Moths.* New York: G. P. Putnam's Sons, 1978.

Peterson, Roger Tory; Pyle, Robert Michael; and Hughes, Sarah Anne. *A Field Guide to Butterflies Coloring Book.* Boston: Houghton Mifflin, 1983.

Pyle, Robert Michael. *Watching Washington Butterflies.* Seattle: Seattle Audubon Society, 1974.

Pyle, Robert Michael. "Conservation of Lepidoptera in the United States." *Biological Conservation* 9 (1976):55–75.

Pyle, Robert Michael. "How to Conserve Insects for Fun and Necessity." *Terra* 17/4 (1979):18–22.

Pyle, Robert Michael. "Butterflies: Now You See Them ..." *International Wildlife,* January/February, 1981.

Pyle, Robert Michael. *The Audubon Society Field Guide to North American Butterflies.* New York: Alfred A. Knopf, 1981.

Pyle, R.; Bentzien, M.; and Opler, P. "Insect Conservation." *Annual Review of Entomology* 26 (1981):233–58.

Schemske, Douglas W. "Pollinator Specificity in *Lantana camara* and *L. trifolia* (Verbenaceae)." *Biotropica* 8/4 (1976):260–264.

Scudder, Samuel Hubbard. *Frail Children of the Air: Excursions Into the World of Butterflies.* Boston: Houghton, Mifflin and Company, 1897.

Shaw, John. "Splendor in the Grass: Tips From a Professional on How to Photograph Insects." *Blair & Ketchum's Country Journal,* June, 1984.

Shepardson, Lucia. *The Butterfly Trees.* San Francisco: The James H. Barry Company, 1914.

Shields, Oakley. "Flower Visitation Records for Butterflies." *The Pan-Pacific Entomologist* 48 (1972):189–203.

Shields, Oakley; Emmel, John F.; and Breedlove, Dennis E. "Butterfly Larval Foodplant Records and a Procedure for Reporting Foodplants." *The Journal of Research on the Lepidoptera* 8/1 (1969–70):21–36.

Singer, Michael C., and Gilbert, Lawrence E. "Ecology of Butterflies in the Urbs and Suburbs." *In Perspectives in Urban Entomology.* New York: Academic Press, 1978.

Smart, Paul. *The Illustrated Encyclopedia of the Butterfly World.* New York: Chartwell Books, 1984.

Sonntag, Linda. *Butterflies.* New York: G.P. Putnam's Sons, 1980.

Struwe, Goran. "Spectral Sensitivity of the Compound Eye in Butterflies (*Heliconius*)." *Journal of Comparative Physiology* 79 (1972):191–96.

Swihart, C.A., and Swihart, S.L. "Colour Selection and Learned Feeding Preferences in the Butterfly, *Heliconius charitonius* Linn." *Animal Behavior* 18 (1970):60–64.

Swihart, Christine A. "Color Discrimination by the Butterfly, *Heliconius charitonius* Linn." *Animal Behaviour* 19 (1971):156–64.

Swihart, S.L. "The Neural Basis of Colour Vision in the Butterfly, *Heliconius erato.*" *Journal of Insect Physiology* 18 (1972):1015–25.

Teale, Edwin Way. *Grassroot Jungles: A Book of Insects.* New York: Dodd, Mead & Company, 1937.

Teale, Edwin Way. "The Journeying Butterflies." *Audubon,* September–October, 1954.

Tekulsky, Mathew. "Butterflies are Free: Where to Go Find Them." *Los Angeles Times, You* magazine, September 27, 1977.

Tietz, Harrison M. *The Lepidoptera of Pennsylvania: A Manual.* State College, PA: The Pennsylvania State College School of Agriculture, Agricultural Experiment Station, 1952.

Tietz, Harrison M. *An Index to the Described Life Histories, Early Stages and Hosts of the Macrolepidoptera of the Continental United States and Canada.* Two volumes. Sarasota, FL: Allyn Museum of Entomology, 1972.

Tilden, J.W. *Butterflies of the San Francisco Bay Region.* Berkeley: University of California Press, 1965.

Tyler, Hamilton A. *The Swallowtail Butterflies of North America.* Healdsburg, CA: Naturegraph Publishers, 1975.

Urguhart, F.A. *The Monarch Butterfly.* Toronto: University of Toronto Press, 1960.

Vane-Wright, Richard I., and Ackery, Phillip R., eds. *The Biology of Butterflies.* In Symposium of the Royal Entomological Society Series. London and Orlando, FL: Academic Press, 1984.

Watson, Allan, and Whalley, Paul E.S. *The Dictionary of Butterflies and Moths in Color.* New York: Simon and Schuster, 1983.

Weed, Clarence M. *Butterflies.* Garden City, NY: Doubleday, Doran & Company, 1926.

Wigglesworth, V.B. *The Life of Insects.* New York: The New American Library, 1968.

Williams, C.B. *The Migration of Butterflies.* Edinburgh and London: Oliver and Boyd, 1930.

Williams, Ted. "Butterflies are Full of Surprises." *National Wildlife,* August–September, 1979.

Zim, Herbert S., and Cottam, Clarence. *Insects.* New York: Golden Press, 1956.

Butterfly Gardening

Anderson, Ethel. "A Garden of Butterflies." *The Atlantic Monthly,* August, 1940.

Atwood, Edna Peck. "Violet Fancier." *Nature Magazine* 46/2 (1953):77–79.

Borkin, Susan Sullivan. "Plant a Butterfly Garden." *Lore* 34/2 (1984):7–11.

Brady, Philip. "Boarding House for Butterflies." *Nature Magazine* 51/4 (1958):188–90.

Brewer, Jo. "How to Attract Butterflies." *Horticulture*, July, 1969.

Brewer, Jo. "An Invitation to the Butterfly Meadow." *Defenders*, August, 1978.

Brewer, Jo. "Bringing Butterflies to the Garden." *Horticulture*, May, 1979.

Brewer, Jo. "Butterfly Gardening." *Xerces Society Self-Help Sheet No. 7,* 1982.

Buck, Margaret Waring. *In Yards and Gardens.* New York: Abingdon Press, 1952.

Cervoni, Cleti. "Butterfly Gardens." *Essex Life,* Spring, 1985.

Collman, Sharon J. "The Butterfly's World: Notes of a Butterfly Gardener." *University of Washington Arboretum Bulletin* 46/2 (1983): 16–26.

Crane, Jocelyn. "Keeping House for Tropical Butterflies." *National Geographic,* August, 1957.

Cribb, Peter. "How to Encourage Butterflies to Live in Your Garden." *Insect Conservation News* (Amateur Entomologists' Society, U.K.) 6 (1982):4–10.

Crotch, W.J.B. "A Silkmoth Rearer's Handbook." *The Amateur Entomologist* 12 (1956):1–165.

Damrosch, Barbara. "A Butterfly Garden." In *Theme Gardens.* New York: Workman Publishing Company, 1982.

Dimock, Thomas E. "Culture Maintenance of *Vanessa atalanta rubria* (Nymphalidae)." *The Journal of Research on the Lepidoptera* 23 (1984):236–40.

Dirig, Robert. *Growing Moths.* Ithaca, NY: New York State College of Agriculture and Life Sciences, Cornell University, 4-H Members' Guide M-6-6, 1975.

Dirig, Robert. "Butterflies, Cabbages and Kids." *Teacher,* May/June, 1976.

Donahue, Julian P. "Take a Butterfly to Lunch: A Guide to Butterfly Gardening in Los Angeles." *Terra* 14/3 (1976):3–12 plus fold-out poster.

Donahue, Julian P. "How to Create a Butterfly Garden." First Day Cover Page. The Reader's Digest Association, Inc., 1977.

Druse, Ken. "Butterflies are Free, But You Can Lure Them to Your Garden With Their Favorite Flowers." *House Beautiful,* August, 1984.

Dun's Business Month. "Butterflies for Sale." May, 1984.

Ginna, Robert Emmett, Jr. "A Shared Passion for Bugs." *Yankee,* September, 1984.

Goodall, Nancy-Mary. "Flowers for Butterflies." *The Illustrated London News,* July, 1978.

Goodden, Robert. "Butterflies of the Garden and Hedgerow." Concertina Publications Limited. In the greeting-card series, "Cards to Keep," 1978.

Green, Timothy. "Beautiful Fliers Fill an Indoor Jungle in Suburban London." *Smithsonian,* January, 1985.

Haas, Carolyn; Cole, Ann; and Naftzger, Barbara. *Backyard Vacation: Outdoor Fun in Your Own Neighborhood*. Boston: Little, Brown, and Company, 1980.

Harrison, George H. "A Farm Full of Butterflies." *Ranger Rick's Nature Magazine,* October, 1982.

Harrison, George H. "Boom Times for Backyard Habitat: How People Are Creating Havens for Wildlife in Their Own Backyards." *National Wildlife,* October–November, 1983.

Hastings, Boyd. "Where Dandelions Grow." *Organic Gardening,* April, 1981.

Headstrom, Richard. *Suburban Wildlife: An Introduction to the Common Animals of Your Back Yard and Local Park*. Englewood Cliffs, NJ: Prentice-Hall, 1984.

Heal, Henry George. "An Experiment in Conservation Education: The Drum Manor Butterfly Garden." *International Journal of Environmental Studies* 4 (1973):223–29.

Howe, William H. "What's in Your Backyard?" *The Lepidopterists' News* 12 (1958):130.

Hult, Ruby El. "Some Notes On My Butterfly Gardening and Butterfly Raising." *Wings* 4/3 (1978) and 5/1 (1978):11.

Jackson, Bernard S. *Butterflies of Oxen Pond Botanic Park*. St. John's, Newfoundland: Memorial University of Newfoundland, 1976.

Jackson, Bernard S. "How to Start a Butterfly Garden." *Nature Canada,* April/June, 1977.

Jackson, Bernard S. "Butterfly Farming in Newfoundland." *Canadian Geographic,* August/September, 1979.

Jackson, Bernard S. "Oxen Pond Botanic Park." *Garden,* November/December, 1981.

Jackson, Bernard S. "The Oxen Pond Botanic Park as a Reserve For Common Native Butterflies." *Atala* 7 (1981):15–22.

Jackson, Bernard S. "The Lowly Dandelion Deserves More Respect." *Canadian Geographic,* June/July, 1982.

Joode, Ton de, and Stolk, Anthonie. "The Butterfly and the Moth." In *The Backyard Bestiary*. New York: Alfred A. Knopf, 1982.

Kulman, H.M. "Butterfly Production Management." *University of Minnesota Agricultural Experiment Station Technical Bulletin* 310 (1977):39–47.

Lutz, Frank E. *A Lot of Insects: Entomology in a Suburban Garden*. New York: G.P. Putnam's Sons, 1941.

Malinsky, Iris. "The Pleasure of Flowers and Butterflies." *Los Angeles Times Home* magazine, December 11, 1977.

Measures, David G. "Butterflies In Your Garden." *Bright Wings of Summer.* Englewood Cliffs, NJ: Prentice-Hall, 1976.

Moran, B.K. "City Butterflies." *San Francisco,* April, 1982.

Morton, Ashley. "The Importance of Farming Butterflies." *New Scientist,* May 20, 1982.

National Wildlife Federation. *Gardening with Wildlife.* Washington, D.C.: NWF, 1974.

Neulieb, Robert and Marilyn. "With Care, You Can Coax Butterflies Into Residence." *The Christian Science Monitor,* June 27, 1982: 15.

Newman, L. Hugh. "When Churchill Brought Butterflies to Chartwell." *Audubon,* May/June, 1965.

Newman, L. Hugh. "Churchill's Interest in Animal Life." *Audubon,* July/August, 1965.

Newman, L. Hugh. *Living With Butterflies.* London: John Baker, 1967.

Newman, L. Hugh, with Savonius, Moira. *Create a Butterfly Garden.* London: John Baker, 1967.

Newsom-Brighton, Maryanne. "Butterflies are Free." *National Wildlife,* April/May, 1982.

Newsom-Brighton, Maryanne. "A Garden of Butterflies." *Organic Gardening,* January, 1983.

Norsgaard, E. Jaediker. "The Lawn That Went Wild." *Ranger Rick's Nature Magazine,* May/June, 1976.

Oates, Matthew. *Garden Plants for Butterflies.* Fareham, Hampshire: Brian Masterson & Associates Limited, 1985.

Oppewall, Jeannine. "History of Butterfly Farming in California." *Terra* 17/4 (1979):30–35.

Owen, Denis F. "Conservation of Butterflies in Garden Habitats." *Environmental Conservation* 3/4 (1976):285–290.

Owen, Denis F. "Insect Diversity in an English Suburban Garden." In *Perspectives in Urban Entomology.* New York: Academic Press, 1978.

Owen, D.F. "Species Diversity in Butterflies in a Tropical Garden." *Biological Conservation* 3/3 (1971): 191–198.

Owen, D.F. "Estimating the Abundance and Diversity of Butterflies." *Biological Conservation* 8 (1975): 173–183.

Owen, Jennifer, and Owen, D.F. "Suburban Gardens: England's Most Important Nature Reserve?" *Environmental Conservation* 2/1 (1975):53–59.

Peattie, Donald Culross. "How to Attract Butterflies to Your Garden." *Better Homes & Gardens,* August, 1941.

Pyle, Robert Michael. "Railways and Butterflies." *Xerces Society Self-Help Sheet* No. 2, 1974.

Pyle, Robert Michael. "Create a Community Butterfly Reserve." *Xerces Society Self-Help Sheet* No. 4, 1975.

Pyle, Robert Michael. "Butterfly Gardening." In *The Audubon Society Handbook for Butterfly Watchers.* New York: Charles Scribner's Sons, 1984.

Ranger Rick's Nature Magazine. "Butterfly Garden." May, 1977.

Reinhard, Harriet V. "Food Plants for Butterflies." California Native Plant Society *Newsletter* 6/4 (1970):3–6.

Rothschild, Miriam and Farrell, Clive. *The Butterfly Gardener.* London: Michael Joseph/Rainbird, 1983.

Simon, Seymour. "Butterflies and Moths." In *Pets in a Jar: Collecting and Caring For Small Wild Animals.* New York: Penguin Books, 1979.

Smith, Alice Upham. "Attracting Butterflies To the Garden." *Horticulture,* August, 1975.

Smith, Jack. "A Passion For Butterflies." *Los Angeles Times, View* section, April 13, 1976.

Smithsonian Magazine, February, 1979. "She Raises Monarchs in Mid-Manhattan."

Stokes, Bruce. "The Urban Garden: A Growing Trend." *Sierra,* July/August, 1978.

Stone, John L.S. and Midwinter, H.J. *Butterfly Culture: A Guide to Breeding Butterflies, Moths, and Other Insects.* Poole, Dorset, UK: Blandford Press, 1975.

Sunset Joy of Gardening 1978. "Attracting Butterflies to Your Garden."

Sunset Magazine, "They Like Only Passion Vines." April, 1961.

Teale, Edwin Way. *Near Horizons: The Story of An Insect Garden.* London: Robert Hale Limited, 1947.

Tekulsky, Mathew. "Butterfly Gardening." *Family Circle Great Ideas,* February, 1983.

Thomas, Jack Ward; Brush, Robert O.; and DeGraaf, Richard M. "Invite Wildlife To Your Backyard." *National Wildlife,* April–May, 1973.

Titlow, Debby Igleheart. "Gardens On the Wing." *Colorado Homes & Lifestyles,* May/June, 1984.

Tylka, David. "Butterfly Gardens." *Missouri Conservationist,* June, 1980.

U.S. Department of the Interior. *Establishing Trails on Rights-of-Way: Principally Railroad Abandonments.* Superintendent of Documents, U.S. Government Printing Office, Washington, D.C.

Vietmeyer, Noel D. "Butterfly Ranching is Taking Wing in Papua New Guinea." *Smithsonian,* May, 1979.

Vietmeyer, Noel D. (ed.) *Butterfly Farming in Papua New Guinea.* Washington, D.C.: National Academy Press, 1983.

Villiard, Paul. *Moths and How to Rear Them.* New York: Funk & Wagnalls, 1969.

Weaver, Mary Anne. "Barely a Flutter At the World's First Walk-through Butterfly Zoo." *The Christian Science Monitor,* February 22, 1985:11.

Williams, Ted. "A Butterfly Garden." *Garden,* July/August, 1980.

Williams, Ted. "How to Plant a Butterfly Garden." *Sanctuary,* April, 1984.

Wiltshire, Lilas. "Informal Garden Helps Lure Butterflies." *Los Angeles Times,* Section 1-A:6, June 8, 1984.

Wolf, Nancy and Guttentag, Roger. "Butterfly Season." *Eco-News,* May, 1975.

Yajima, Minoru. "The Insectarium at Tama Zoo, Tokyo." *International Zoo Yearbook* 12 (1972):96.

Xerces Society. "Butterfly Gardening—One Way to Increase Urban Wildlife (California Edition)" *Xerces Society Educational Leaflet,* 1978, No. 2.

Flowers and Gardening

Baker, Herbert G. and Irene. "Some Anthecological Aspects of the Evolution of Nectar-producing Flowers, Particularly Amino Acid Production in Nectar." In *Taxonomy and Ecology.* London: Academic Press, 1973.

Baker, Herbert G. and Hurd, Paul D., Jr. "Intrafloral Ecology." *Annual Review of Entomology* 13(1968):385–414.

Brockman, C. Frank. *Trees of North America.* New York: Golden Press, 1968.

Bruce, Hal. *How to Grow Wildflowers and Wild Shrubs and Trees in Your Own Garden.* New York: Alfred A. Knopf, 1976.

Craighead, John J.; Craighead, Frank C., Jr.; and Davis, Ray J. *A Field Guide to Rocky Mountain Wildflowers.* Boston: Houghton Mifflin, 1963.

Crockett, James Underwood. *Annuals.* New York: Time-Life Books, 1973.

Crockett, James Underwood. *Perennials.* New York: Time-Life Books, 1973.

Crockett, James Underwood and Allen, Oliver E. *Wildflower Gardening.* Alexandria, VA: Time-Life Books, 1977.

Dana, Mrs. William Starr. *How to Know the Wild Flowers.* Revised and edited by Clarence J. Hylander. New York: Dover Publications, 1963. (Originally published New York: Charles Scribner's Sons, 1900.)

Faegri, K. and Pijl, L. van der. *The Principles of Pollination Ecology.* Oxford: Pergamon Press, 1979.

Grant, Verne and Karen A. *Flower Pollination in the Phlox Family.* New York: Columbia University Press, 1965.

Headstrom, Richard. *Suburban Wildflowers: An Introduction to the Common Wild-flowers of Your Back Yard and Local Park.* Englewood Cliffs, NJ: Prentice-Hall, 1984.

Hersey, Jean. *The Woman's Day Book of Wildflowers.* New York: Simon and Schuster, 1976.

Hull, Helen S. *Wild Flowers for Your Garden.* New York: Gramercy Publishing Company, 1952.

Kevan, Peter G. "Pollination and Environmental Conservation." *Environmental Conservation* 2/4 (1975):293–98.

Knuth, Dr. Paul. *Handbook of Flower Pollination: Based Upon Hermann Muller's Work 'The Fertilisation of Flowers by Insects.'* (Volume 1: Introduction and Literature). Oxford: The Clarendon Press, 1906.

Kruckeberg, Arthur R. *Gardening with Native Plants of the Pacific Northwest.* Seattle: University of Washington Press, 1982.

Lacy, Allen. "Butterfly Weed." In *Home Ground: A Gardener's Miscellany.* New York: Farrar, Straus and Giroux, 1984.

Meeuse, Bastiaan and Morris, Sean. *The Sex Life of Flowers.* New York: Facts on File, 1984.

Muller, Hermann. *The Fertilisation of Flowers.* London: Macmillan and Co., 1883.

Niehaus, Theodore F. *A Field Guide to Pacific States Wildflowers.* Boston: Houghton Mifflin, 1976.

Peterson, Roger Tory and McKenny, Margaret. *A Field Guide to Wildflowers: Northeastern and North-central North America.* Rev. ed. Boston: Houghton Mifflin Harcourt, 1998.

Proctot, Michael and Yeo, Peter. *The Pollination of Flowers.* London: Collins, 1973.

Ray, Mary Helen and Nicholls, Robert P., eds. *A Guide to Significant & Historic Gardens of America.* Athens, GA: Agee Publishers, 1983.

Richards, A.J., ed. *The Pollination of Flowers by Insects.* London and Orlando, Fl.: Academic Press, Linnean Society Symposium Series No. 6, 1978.

Ruggiero, Michael A. *Spotter's Guide to Wild Flowers of North America.* New York: Mayflower Books, 1979.

Sinnes, A. Cort. *All About Annuals.* San Francisco: Ortho Books, 1981.

Sinnes, A. Cort. *All About Perennials.* San Francisco: Ortho Books, 1981.

Spellenberg, Richard. *National Audubon Society Field Guide to North American Wildflowers: Western Region.* Rev. ed. New York: Alfred A. Knopf, 2001.

Spencer, Edwin Rollin. *All About Weeds.* New York: Dover Publications, 1974.

Sperka, Marie. *Growing Wildflowers: A Gardener's Guide.* New York: Charles Scribner's Sons, 1984.

Steffek, Edwin F. *The New Wild Flowers and How to Grow Them*. Beaverton, OR: Timber Press, 1983.

Sunset Books. *Color in Your Garden*. Menlo Park, CA: Lane Publishing Co., 1975.

Taylor, Kathryn S. and Hamblin, Stephen F. *Handbook of Wild Flower Cultivation*. New York: The Macmillan Company, 1963.

Tenenbaum, Frances. *Gardening with Wild Flowers*. New York: Charles Scribner's Sons, 1973.

The New Sunset Western Garden Book. New York: Oxmoor House, 2012.

Thieret, John W., Niering, William A., and Olmstead, Nancy C. *National Audubon Society Field Guide to North American Wildflowers: Eastern Region*. Rev. ed. New York: Alfred A. Knopf, 2001.

United States Department of Agriculture. *Common Weeds of the United States*. New York: Dover Publications, 1971.

Zim, Herbert S. and Martin, Alexander C. *Flowers*. New York: Golden Press.

About the Photographs

All of the photographs were taken with a Canon EOS 7D camera.

Page: x. Zebra Heliconian, Los Angeles, CA, 8/11/14
Canon 180mm macro lens, ISO 1250, 1/500 second at f/8
The Zebra Heliconian is a good example of a longwing butterfly.

Page: 1. Monarch, Los Angeles, CA, 8/22/14
Canon 60mm macro lens, ISO 1250, 1/640 second at f/5
The Monarch is the quintessential butterfly.

Page: 4. Giant Swallowtail, Los Angeles, CA, 8/21/14
Canon 180mm macro lens, ISO 1000, 1/1600 second at f/5
The Giant Swallowtail uses its proboscis to drink nectar.

Page: 11 (top). Gulf Fritillary, Pasadena, CA, 7/5/12
Canon 100-400mm lens at 310mm, ISO 800, 1/1250 second at f/5.6
The Gulf Fritillary, showing its upperside and underside.

Page: 11 (bottom). Anise Swallowtail, Los Angeles, CA, 7/8/14
Canon 50mm macro lens, ISO 800, 1/1600 second at f/5.6
The Anise Swallowtail features a great combination of colors.

Page: 12. Checkered White, Los Angeles, CA, 8/4/14
Canon 180mm macro lens, ISO 1000, 1/3200 second at f/7.1
The Checkered White, here on lantana, is common in many neighborhoods.

Page: 14. Giant Swallowtails, Santa Barbara, CA, 8/23/14
Canon 18-135mm lens at 135mm, ISO 1000, 1/2500 second at f/5.6
What a treat to see two Giant Swallowtails at the same star clusters flower head.

Page: 16 (top). Orange-barred Sulphur, Santa Barbara, CA, 9/6/14
Canon 100mm macro lens, ISO 1000, 1/2500 second at f.7.1
This Orange-barred Sulphur looks magnificent.

Page: 16 (bottom). Julia Heliconian, Los Angeles, CA, 7/3/14
Canon 50mm macro lens, ISO 400, 1/2500 second at f/4
The Julia Heliconian has long, narrow wings.

Page: 20. Monarch laying an egg, Los Angeles, CA, 8/21/14
Canon 180mm macro lens, ISO 800, 1/800 second at f/8
The Monarch female lays an egg on the underside of a milkweed leaf…

Page: 21 (top). Monarch egg, Los Angeles, CA, 8/21/14
Canon 180mm macro lens, ISO 800, 1/2500 second at f/6.3
…and here is that egg.

Page: 21 (bottom). Pipevine Swallowtail eggs, Los Angeles, CA, 8/22/14
Canon 60mm macro lens, ISO 1250, 1/2500 second at f/4
The Pipevine Swallowtail lays its eggs in clusters.

Page: 23. Anise Swallowtail caterpillar, Los Angeles, CA, 7/8/14
Canon 50mm macro lens, ISO 640, 1/320 second at f/10
The Anise Swallowtail caterpillar feeds on a fennel leaf.

Page: 24. Monarch caterpillar, Los Angeles, CA, 8/11/14
Canon 180mm macro lens, ISO 4000, 1/1000 second at f/7.1
The Monarch caterpillar munches on a milkweed plant.

Page: 25 (top). Monarch chrysalis, Los Angeles, CA, 8/21/14
Canon 180mm macro lens, 2000 ISO, 1/2500 second at f/5.6
The Monarch chrysalis, with its gold spots, is like a jeweled pendant.

Page: 25 (bottom). Anise Swallowtail chrysalis, Los Angeles, CA, 8/11/14
Canon 50mm macro lens, ISO 1000, 1/1000 second at f/6.3
The Anise Swallowtail chrysalis uses a silk thread to hold itself in place.

Page: 28 (top). Western Tiger Swallowtail, Los Angeles, CA, 8/11/14
Canon 180mm macro lens, ISO 1250, 1/8000 second at f/3.5
The Western Tiger Swallowtail drinks some nectar at a Cape plumbago flower head…

Page: 28 (bottom). Western Tiger Swallowtail, Los Angeles, CA, 8/11/14
Canon 180mm macro lens, ISO 1250, 1/8000 at f/3.5
…and then rises up into the sky.

Page: 32. Common Buckeye, Santa Barbara, CA, 9/6/14
Canon 100mm macro lens, ISO 1000, 1/400 second at f/10
The Common Buckeye's eyespots attract predators away from its vital organs.

Page: 33. Viceroy, Calais, VT, 7/31/12
Canon 18–135mm lens at 135mm, ISO 640, 1/640 second at f/10
The Viceroy mimics the Monarch, which is distasteful to predators.

Page: 36. Gulf Fritillary, Pasadena, CA, 7/5/14
Canon 100–400mm lens at 400mm, ISO 800, 1/2000 second at f/5.6
The Gulf Fritillary, here on purpletop vervain, is awash in color in this image.

Page: 38 (top). Cabbage White, Los Angeles, CA, 8/13/14
Canon 180mm macro lens, ISO 1600, 1/3200 second at f/8
The Cabbage White, here on lavender in my garden, is a widespread species.

Page: 38 (bottom). Queen, Los Angeles, CA, 8/11/14
Canon 180mm macro lens, ISO 1250, 1/1250 second at f/6.3
The Queen is closely related to the Monarch.

Page: 40 (top). Polydamas Swallowtail, Los Angeles, CA, 8/11/14
Canon 180mm macro lens, ISO 1250, 1/2000 second at f/4.5
The Polydamas Swallowtail has a great combination of black and yellow.

Page: 40 (bottom). Zebra Heliconian, Los Angeles, CA, 7/8/14
Canon 50mm macro lens, ISO 500, 1/500 second at f/8
The Zebra Heliconian has a soft, lilting flight.

Page: 41. Palamedes Swallowtail, Santa Barbara, CA, 8/23/14
Canon 180mm macro lens, ISO 1600, 1/5000 second at f/4.5
The Palamedes Swallowtail is a denizen of swamplands.

Page: 42. Common Wood-Nymph, Calais, VT, 7/17/12
Canon 18–135mm lens at 135mm, ISO 320, 1/400 second at f/8
The Common Wood-Nymph likes open, grassy areas.

Page: 44. Giant Swallowtail, Los Angeles, CA, 8/11/14
Canon 180mm macro lens, ISO 1250, 1/2000 second at f/5
The Giant Swallowtail is a majestic butterfly.

Page: 45. Southern Dogface, Los Angeles, CA, 7/8/14
Canon 50mm macro lens, ISO 800, 1/1600 second at f/5.6
The Southern Dogface enjoys a drink.

Page: 46 (top). Painted Lady, Calais, VT, 7/27/12
Canon 18-135mm lens at 135mm, ISO 800, 1/500 second at f/9
The Painted Lady can be seen in gardens throughout the world.

Page: 46 (bottom). Cloudless Sulphur, Santa Barbara, CA, 8/23/14
Canon 180mm macro lens, ISO 800, 1/2500 second at f/4.5
The Cloudless Sulphur presents a nice profile.

Page: 47. Great Southern White, Los Angeles, CA, 8/11/14
Canon 180mm macro lens, ISO 1000, 1/1250 second at f/5
The Great Southern White, here on Mexican heather, is distinguished by its turquoise antennal clubs.

Page: 49. Gulf Fritillary, Los Angeles, CA, 8/21/14
Canon 180mm macro lens, ISO 1000, 1/4000 second at f/4
The Gulf Fritillary, as seen from below.

Page: 50. Cabbage White, Los Angeles, CA, 8/13/14
Canon 180mm macro lens, ISO 1250, 1/3200 second at f/6.3
The Cabbage White hangs out on a leaf in my garden.

Page: 59. Common Buckeye, Los Angeles, CA, 7/8/14
Canon 50mm macro lens, ISO 500, 1/1000 second at f/4.5
The Common Buckeye, as seen from below.

Page: 60. Zebra Heliconian (foreground) and White Peacock (background), Santa Barbara, CA, 8/23/14
Canon 180mm macro lens, ISO 1600, 1/800 second at f/9
These two species exemplify the great variety of butterfly shapes and colors.

Page: 62 (top). Pipevine Swallowtail (foreground) and Monarch (background),
  Santa Barbara, CA, 8/23/14
Canon 180mm macro lens, ISO 1250, 1/3200 second at f/4
This Pipevine Swallowtail shares a flower patch with a Monarch.

Page: 62 (bottom). White Peacock, Santa Barbara, CA, 8/23/14
Canon 180mm macro lens, ISO 1250, 1/4000 second at f/4
The White Peacock perches on a flower platform.

Page: 64 (top). Gulf Fritillary, Pasadena, CA, 7/5/14
Canon 100-400mm lens at 400mm, ISO 500, 1/1600 second at f/5.6
The silver spots on the underside of the Gulf Fritillary are spectacular.

Page: 64 (bottom). Julia Heliconian, Los Angeles, CA,
  7/8/14
Canon 50mm macro lens, ISO 800, 1/800 second at f/7.1
The Julia Heliconian shares a flower head with a ladybug.

Page: 66. Polydamas Swallowtail, Los Angeles, CA, 8/11/14
Canon 180mm macro lens, ISO 4000, 1/8000 second at f/4
The Polydamas Swallowtail flutters its wings as it drinks nectar.

Page: 68. Monarch, Los Angeles, CA, 8/22/14
Canon 60mm macro lens, ISO 1000, 1/1000 second at f/4.5
The Monarch uses milkweed as a nectar source and larval foodplant.

Page: 74. Gulf Fritillary (left) and Julia Heliconian (right), Santa Barbara, CA,
  9/6/14
Canon 100mm macro lens, ISO 800, 1/2000 second at f/5.6
*The Gulf Fritillary and Julia Heliconian, perched on slices of orange and cantaloupe
  respectively.*

Page: 76. Gulf Fritillary, Pasadena, CA, 7/5/14
Canon 100-400mm lens at 400mm, ISO 500, 1/1600 second at f/5.6
The Gulf Fritillary perches in order to drink nectar from the flowers.

Page: 81. Orange-barred Sulphur, Santa Barbara, CA, 8/23/14
Canon 180mm macro lens, ISO 1600, 1/3200 second at f/4
The Orange-barred Sulphur clings to a sage flower.

Page: 83. Western Tiger Swallowtail, Los Angeles, CA, 8/31/14
Canon 60mm macro lens, ISO 800, 1/800 second at f/5.6
The Western Tiger Swallowtail perches delicately as it drinks in my garden.

Page: 84 (top). Cabbage White, Los Angeles, CA, 8/13/14
Canon 180mm macro lens, ISO 1600, 1/2500 second at f/6.3
The Cabbage White is a regular visitor to my garden.

Page: 84 (bottom). Marine Blue, Los Angeles, CA, 7/26/14
Canon 180mm macro lens, ISO 1000, 1/4000 second at f/8
The Marine Blue on a rose in my garden.

Page: 85. Gray Hairstreak, Los Angeles, CA, 8/5/14
Canon 180mm macro lens, ISO 1250, 1/3200 second at f/8
The Gray Hairstreak, here in my garden, is widespread throughout North America.

Page: 86. Umber Skipper, Los Angeles, CA, 8/5/14
Canon 180mm macro lens, ISO 1250, 1/2500 second at f/9
The Umber Skipper in my garden, with its coiled proboscis.

Page: 92. Gulf Fritillary, Santa Barbara, CA, 8/23/14
Canon 180mm macro lens, ISO 1250, 1/800 second at f/8
The Gulf Fritillary brightens up any garden.

Page: 94. Cabbage White, Los Angeles, CA, 8/13/14
Canon 180mm macro lens, ISO 1250, 1/3200 second at f/5.6
This Cabbage White entertained me for about forty minutes in my garden.

Page: 101. Gulf Fritillary, Pasadena, CA, 7/5/14
Canon 100-400mm lens at 400mm, ISO 1000, 1/2000 second at f/5.6
The sun shines through the wings of this backlit Gulf Fritillary.

Page: 102 (top). Giant Swallowtail, Santa Barbara, CA, 8/23/14
Canon 180mm macro lens, ISO 1250, 1/1600 second at f/5
Looking up at the Giant Swallowtail makes an interesting composition.

Page: 102 (bottom). Great Southern White, Santa Barbara, CA, 9/6/14
Canon 100mm macro lens, ISO 1000, 1/2000 second at f/4.5
Backlighting creates an ethereal effect with this Great Southern White.

Page: 103. Spicebush Swallowtail, Santa Barbara, CA, 9/6/14
Canon 100mm macro lens, ISO 800, 1/2500 second at f/4
The Spicebush Swallowtail mimics the Pipevine Swallowtail, which is distasteful to predators.

Page: 104. Orange-barred Sulphur, Santa Barbara, CA, 9/6/14
Canon 100mm macro lens, ISO 1000, 1/8000 second at f/2.8
The Orange-barred Sulphur features a gorgeous shade of yellow.

Page: 112. Atala (foreground) and Monarch (background), Santa Barbara, CA, 8/23/14
Canon 180mm macro lens, ISO 1600, 1/8000 second at f/3.5
The Atala and the Monarch are a beautiful study in contrasts.

Page: 115. Atala, Santa Barbara, CA, 8/23/14
Canon 60mm macro lens, ISO 1250, 1/1250 second at f/4.5
The black, blue, and red colors of the Atala make it distinctive.

Page: 117. Monarch, Los Angeles, CA, 8/11/14
Canon 180mm macro lens, ISO 1600, 1/2000 second at f/4
The Monarch finds an open flower.

Page: 118. Left to right: Queen, Common Buckeye, and Monarch, Santa Barbara, CA, 8/23/14
Canon 50mm macro lens, ISO 1000, 1/1000 second at f/8
The Queen, Common Buckeye, and Monarch perch on a flower together.

Index